Life is Change
Growth is Optional

KAREN KAISER CLARK

Life is Change
Growth is Optional

KAREN KAISER CLARK
ILLUSTRATIONS BY LARRY W. ANDERSON

Karen Kaiser Clark

2·12·1999

The Center for Executive Planning, Inc.
13119 Heritage Way – Suite 1200
St. Paul, Minnesota 55124
Telephone (612) 454-1163

Second Printing,. December 1996

Clark, Karen Kaiser, 1942
  Life is Change – Growth is Optional
  Illustrated by Larry W. Anderson
  Cover design by Jennifer Haas
  LCN: 93-90023

  ISBN: 0-9626467-2-5

Other Books in The Trilogy of Growth Series by Karen Kaiser Clark
Published by The Center for Executive Planning, Inc.

"Where Have All The Children Gone?
Gone to Grown-Ups, Everyone!"

"Grow Deep – Not Just Tall"

DEDICATION

This book is dedicated to you, My Friend, and to all of our sisters and brothers. May the wise and weathered oak nurture us towards choosing to grow through all of the changes and seasons of our lives. May the strength of her example empower us to make a healing difference in our world. May her story prompt us to listen to the Spirit who speaks uniquely to each of us and to see, My Friend, that we are indeed all members of one sacred forest family!

"Then I was standing on the highest mountain of them all. All around about beneath me was the whole hoop of the world. And while I stood there, I saw more than I can tell and I understood more than I saw, for I was seeing in a sacred manner the shapes of all things in the spirit and the shape of all shapes as they must live together like one being. And I saw that the sacred hoop of my people was one of many hoops that made one circle, wide as daylight and as starlight. And in the center grew one mighty flowering tree to shelter all the children of one mother and one father. And I saw that it was holy."

– The Words of Black Elk

One of the many stories of The Sacred Tree

CONTENTS

ACKNOWLEDGEMENTS

In the words of my mother, Kathryn Kaiser, "You cannot put an old head on young shoulders." My appreciation of her and her insights have increased especially as my children, Kelli and Kevin, have grown and my mother is no longer with us. As my shoulders have aged like the branches of the oak, I have come to treasure more dearly those who nurtured my roots. I have also come to appreciate those familiar sayings that revealed great truths in profound simplicity. For your words and for all of you who had faith in me, I thank you.

Time can be our teacher, an instructor of insight, a mentor of mellowed wisdom. I especially wish to express my respect and gratitude for my grandmothers, for my mother-in-law, Mildred Clark, and for all those weathered spirits who believed in the dawn and who modeled compassion. Through their examples I learned that difficult times can become our greatest seasons of growth . . . if . . . we choose to make them so, if we choose to stay meaningfully connected, if we choose to work through our anger and grief, and if we seek more than "justice" and risk to love again.

It has taken seven years to complete this manuscript that reveals my own personal struggle to grow, to find "meaning" and a way to become "more" in the face of change and misfortune. Special thanks is due my husband, Lou, for his continued support and the faithful companionship of all of you who have proven to be all-seasons-friends.

So many people have kindly extended themselves to me in a multitude of ways that I hesitate to try to name them for fear of an innocent omission. I hope that each of you knows personally my deepest gratitude for the gift of your presence in my life. We are indeed all members of one sacred forest family, the children of one Mother Earth.

I wish to thankfully acknowledge Earnie Larson for allowing me to use his words "What we live we learn . . ." Deepest gratitude is also due Renee Fajardo. She wrote the poem "The Gift" for me in thanks for my friendship and granted her permission for its inclusion in this book.

Finally, I wish to acknowledge heartfelt gratitude to all of you Believers in Life who make a healing difference in our world. May we never underestimate the power of even our brief encounters, the influence of our examples, the integral connections we share with one another, and our potential to become more in response to the changing seasons of our lives . . . if . . . we choose TO GROW.

PREFACE

This is the third book in The Trilogy of Growth. The first book was titled, *Where Have All The Children Gone? Gone to Grown-Ups, Everyone!* Written through the eyes of a child, we discovered that life and maturity are more about changes and choices and less about answers and control. We found that the Forever Child within us never goes away. Life calls us to nurture that child deep inside as well as to learn from our elders who have seasoned wisdom to share. Becoming a genuine grown-up requires risking to grow deep.

The second book was titled, *Grow Deep, Not Just Tall*, a quote from the first book. Through the eyes of an oak tree, we journeyed through the four symbolic seasons of the year. We discovered there is potential for growth in every season and in every event. Each must decide how growth will or will not take root in response to what is experienced.

Life is Change – Growth is Optional, completes the trilogy. The title is a quote from the second book. In response to unchosen changes and storms that threaten to destroy her, the oak tree grows even deeper, not just taller. She tells how The Night Winds of Winter ripped her oldest branch from her, but their force did not topple the oak. Sustained by Mother Earth, the oak survives and chooses to risk to grow through her pain.

Only a few months later, The Wind Shear of Summer shattered the oak's most beloved branch, the one that connected her to the cord of life. The force of those unfair winds nearly broke her spirit. Nonetheless, her hope was not extinguished and the oak continues to survive and to grow.

In response to her losses, the oak has struggled to become "more" and not less. In searching for ways to grow through adversity, she has learned to ask for help. She has rerooted and has rediscovered her own lost, abandoned acorn, her own Forever Child. Now with renewed courage, she risks to reach out and to embrace life again. She accepts that storms will likely return, and that they will probably break her heart, not just her branches, if she risks to love again. This is her choice, for she chooses to live life to the fullest.

With symbolism, hope and gentle humor, the oak tree invites you, My Friend, to discover how you too might grow through stormy seasons and embrace your own lost Forever Child. She encourages you to become a Believer in Life who continues to risk, to love, and to grow in response to the challenge of change. She welcomes you to share in the journey as we cycle through the seasons and strive to find new meaning in our ever-changing lives. The worn and weathered oak encourages you to accept that, *Life is Change – Growth is Optional*. She concludes, "Choose wisely, My Friend, and risk to grow!"

SECTION I

REFLECTIONS
ON THE SEASONS

Welcome back, My Friend. I have missed you in the seasons that have separated us. Storms have weathered my spirit and seasoned my soul since we were last together. Often I thought of you. Often I wondered if you thought of me. Yes, even trees get lonely and long to be remembered.

Come close now and lean on me. Let me feel the softness of your cheek gently brush my bending trunk. Let me too lean on you. Vulnerability, not just strength, is what true friendships share. Some of our needs are still out of season. Some of our wounds still ache to be healed. So many buds await to be blossomed through this, our special reunion. Oh, there is so much for us to share! Listen with your heart, My Friend, as I risk to speak to you through mine.

I am a very changed tree than when we were last together. Sudden storms threatened to destroy me. Cruel winds cut through me. There were times when I feared despair would consume me. However, over time those same slashing storms have broadened my vision and deepened my roots. Faithfully, Mother Earth has journeyed with me and I have finally found my way home. Hope's flame once again glows warmly in the heart of my hearth, and I continue to learn how to kindle its spark.

It was the child in you, My Friend, that always so delighted me. I see you have held fast to that magic center of who you are. I am equally delighted to tell you, I have rediscovered my own lost abandoned acorn, the seed of my soul. Now this Forever Child within me speaks directly and I have learned to listen.

I have fewer answers than when we were last together. Experiences have taught me to remain open and continue to question. Life has opened my ears to hear the voices of my elders and those with seasoned-wisdom. Mother Earth has led me to reason with my heart not only with my head. Today the seasons hold new meanings as do moments and memories and you. Now I see that, *Life is Change – Growth is Optional*. Let me explain . . .

My Friend, when life goes smoothly, the sun rises and sets in rhythms rarely noticed. Although the signs of change are forever around us, they are only casually acknowledged as the sun gradually glides higher and lower on the horizon. Days wind into weeks. The full moon squeezes into a thin slice of dull reflections. Suddenly we realize that the light was dimmed and time has escaped us. Yet, it doesn't seem to matter. Our focus is forward with so many days ahead and certainly countless sunrises to brighten the darkness. There is no sense of urgency or need to address hard questions.

Life is orderly. Transitions are smooth. Days predictably proceed as we move through routines we take for granted. Pages are folded back on the calender, marked with chosen memories and moments we "want" to carry into the future. It is all so comfortable, so familiar.

Life feels like forever with plenty of time ahead to say or to do what we now only dream of or dare to imagine. Little fanfare marks the passage of one season slipping away and another arriving. Still, each season is unique, and one is often more favored than the others.

Autumn, The Season of Letting Go and of Growth, used to be my favorite season. For me it was a time to celebrate and to happily harvest what Mother Earth had given. It was a time we trees willingly let go of worn and withered leaves in colorful, joyful, farewell breezes. It was the season of harmonies around bonfires, and a time to prepare for soft white snowflakes and delicate filigrees of frost to adorn our tiniest twigs.

Do you remember, My Friend, how excitedly I used to anticipate Autumn? Openly I reached out my branches to embrace the flocks of chattering travelers. I was anxious to hear of their plans for journeys to longer days. Together we laughed and relished the warm sun that gentled cooler days. We pledged mutual assuredness

that through the Winter we would grow patient in our times of separation. We believed that Spring would surely find us celebrating new beginnings together.

Then one year it didn't work out that way and my favorite season, like EVERYTHING else in my world, CHANGED! Autumn was no longer a joyful time of harmony. There was no celebrating what Mother Earth offered and I harvested what I never would have hoped.

I no longer chose to let go of my leaves. They were twisted and torn by turbulent winds. There was no time to prepare. I was at the mercy of unchosen change and forced to live "letting go and growth" in ways I never dared imagine. The meaning of Autumn was dramatically redefined. Suddenly I realized that a lifetime could be transformed in one single second and that "it" does not happen only to "others." Injustice and change had overwhelmed me! Time from then on was marked as before and after "what happened." Moments became monumental.

Oh, My Friend, easy answers and absolutes from then on have all been questioned. Yesterday is no longer casually tucked away. Tomorrow has lost its guarantee. Trust is fragile. Very little is taken for granted and NOW has become most important. There were seemingly endless times, My Friend, when mere survival was my

whole focus. Often I thought of you and wondered if you ever thought of me.

What a joy, My Friend, this is to find that I was not forgotten. You did remember and you have returned to one who truly loves you. Long ago we shared pieces of our histories and we trusted in each other. You knew and you remember both my branches that are gone. Now we can journey toward the future side-by-side with one another. Today is indeed, a cause for celebration!

Oh, My Friend, be aware of a changed and spirited tree that welcomes you home. These eyes that embrace you have shed more tears than I believed was bearable. My trunk you touch is bent and scarred by winds that lashed and stripped me. My roots that sprawl beneath your feet are deeper and reinvested. I am a very changed tree.

It is hard to know just where to begin, to explain who I have become. Perhaps it would be helpful to recall the lessons we learned from each of the seasons when we were last together. Then I will share how profoundly reordered my world has become since storms of injustice reshaped me. Yes, My Friend, *Life is Change – Growth is Optional*. I have chosen to grow in the face of misfortune.

New life is birthed by shedding old skins and pressing through the darkness towards the light. Spring is The Season of New Beginnings and of Growth. It is the season that teaches us there is potential for growth in every experience, every moment, and even new beginnings in the endings of things.

We must invite the warming sun of Springtime to gradually thaw and expose any painful, early rootings or calloused, worn seed-coverings. Otherwise, they can keep us frozen in rigid routines, narrow visions and painful past experience. In order to grow, WE MUST CHANGE!

Nurturing new beginnings can be frightening. Often it is painful. Fear, like frost, forever threatens to nip the tiny, new buds that hunger for warmth and light. It often feels safer to stay in icy, dark places, than risk unknown blossoms that "might" be born in days to come. Even if we are cold and miserable, at least our world is known and predictable.

Thrusting our imagination too far forward can hurl us into the grip of anxiety. New life and new beginnings are born one moment, one breath, one cautious step at a time. Growth takes time. There are pieces of Winter's patience in new Springtime beginnings. No season stands self-sufficient and all alone. Nor do you or I, My Friend!

Birds need nests and so do we to hatch new life alive. Solid nests are sheltering places where we can weather life's storms. Safe nests need no locks or latches. They are mended with new grasses when they are torn and lined with trusted twigs and supple leaves. Wise are those who build their nests in stable places and with those who will not drop or possess them.

Those who have not known nests that protected and nurtured are especially fearful of risking new beginnings. Trust like an egg shell is easily shattered and when broken too early can leave little birds extra fragile. Still, they can survive and one day they may soar. The most heroic and admirable becomings often have the most humble, vulnerable beginnings. Connecting with Believers in Life can strengthen weary wings.

Believers in Life weather the windstorms and speak quiet truths through example. They mentor beginnings and nurture becomings. Having grown beyond survival, they teach us that "Whenever we lose we gain and whenever we gain we lose." Beginning to understand this marks the budding of insights that can blossom into real courage.

Until we can accept this, we live like little birds clinging to illusive limbs of security, struggling to survive the

Springtime storms. Believing life is assured only by grasping more tightly, we dare not even imagine what might happen if we risked releasing our grip. Yes, there are also pieces of Autumn's letting go in Springtime new beginnings.

If we refuse to risk, we deny ourselves the discovery of unimagined gifts. However, life has a way of shoving us off our perch and we may be utterly amazed to find we have wings and we CAN fly. By releasing a restricted perception of self, we gain an empowered perspective. However, unlike tiny birds, these discoveries are not so spontaneous for us!

Discovering the "gifts" in Springtime lightning gives birth to expanded vision. Like all we experience, lightning can be frightening or brightening, depending upon our perspective. Truth is often hidden. It hints and hungers to be found. Life and love play hide-and-seek everywhere we turn. Not all eyes that are open can see. Worms, the tillers of the soil, are beauty-full in the eyes of Mother Earth. So are we!

My Friend, inconsequential meetings are rare. Do not underestimate the impact of your touch. Seek wisely to connect in meaning-full ways with wide-eyed seekers of truth, those who are willing to begin again, and again and again. This is, Spring, The Season of New Beginnings and of Growth.

Growth never completes itself. Nor does love. Nor do we. Summer, The Season of Fullness and of Growth, teaches us to reach for more than absolute arrivals. It nudges us to grow beyond momentary completeness. To imagine we can have it all, do it all or be it all is a fantasy. This pursuit of the ultimate is at the core of much frustrated unhappiness.

No relationship totally fulfills us. No one is the completion of another. Doomed to disappointment are those who try to fill their emptiness by absorbing another. Rarely is the ultimate a prolonged realization. The climaxing pinnacle of any season is inevitably brushed away with one sweep of a second hand.

"The sun may shine longer in the Summer but the moon still touches everyday." To approach fullness, one must be willing to be touched by all parts of the whole. One cannot know fully the brightness of the sun at high noon without having known the total darkness of a moonless midnight.

Living fully is not an isolated experience. It is an arduous adventure meant to be shared. It is a journey of discovering one's own unique path that undulates with some and clashes with others. It is not about arrivals. It is all about discoveries.

Living fully is not about finding all the right answers and knowing "the" truth. It is all about asking the right questions and discovering "many truths," one at a time. It is a voyage through an ocean of experiences, a striving to keep on keel, a yearning for that fragile balance between giving and receiving, between listening and revealing. It is searching for one tree in the forest and finding a forest in one tree.

The journey within is the longest and most awesome. We discover pieces and potentials of all those we admire and abhor within the essence of ourselves. This journey toward self-discovery is often a lonely trip. Gradually we realize we will never be completely known or understood by any in the forest or even by ourselves. Only Mother Earth knows the whole of Her creation. It can also be a thrilling adventure. Eventually we discover that we are so wonder-full that we are uniquely beyond imagination. Yes, we are mystery as well as matter. We are pieces as well as whole puzzles.

My Friend, do you remember the squirrels? They helped me to come to know and to accept a fuller sense of myself. They playfully invited me to see there is no real living without laughter and loving. Each requires risking the sting of ridicule and rejection. Their gentle humor helped soothe the sting of risks gone awry. Their unconditional acceptance dispelled the need to hide the tears of hurt and sadness.

The squirrels taught me how to play and to have fun. Only those with the faith of the Forever Child truly know how to play. Without The Child, one must constantly work, worry, and strive to contain and control. Play is natural and joy-full exhilaration. It makes no demands and has no desires to succeed or to win, to defeat or demean. The goal of genuine play is simply to enjoy.

A full life makes play a priority. It takes notice of the play-fulness of nature; twinkling stars, bouncing bunnies, winking owls, and flirting fireflies. Perhaps play is a pre-view of paradise; time vanishes, insecurities disappear and joyous fulfillment prevails.

Remember, My Friend, it is the little things that mark the major differences in the larger picture of life. We learned in *Grow Deep, Not Just Tall*, that to live fully is to discover the value of simple pleasures, the importance of rela-tionships, the gift of imagination and the power of hope and love.

To live Summer, The Season of Fullness and of Growth, is to reach out to embrace the whole of life. It requires a will-ingness to accept that there are few lifetime guarantees or successes without price. Those who live this season are willing to risk the full range of feelings, thoughts and imaginings and ever-expanding limits.

Autumn, The Season of Letting Go and of Growth, is as unpredictable as is life. One day resembles a sweltering Summer's afternoon. The next feels like a bone-chilling Winter's dawn. Fall is an exchange of opposites with little or no warning. Autumn reminds us we hold nothing forever, even what we believe we cannot live without . . . and yet we must . . . and we do!

How well I have learned, My Friend, that change, especially sudden change, is typically unchosen. Often it is costly. The insecurity it spurs is unsettling. In striving to camouflage our anxieties, we robe ourselves in the costumes of absolute confidence and control. Risking to expose our vulnerability can be terrifying. However, the masquerade often is ending with an inevitable, sometimes sudden, change of climate. Autumn leaves teach us that the light of truth or the lack of light, in time, reveal our true colors. Neither chlorophyll or camouflage last indefinitely.

Autumn leaves are like tears, tossed and tumbling down in a flood of feelings, often too brittle, too broken for words. The language of tears is spoken with differing accents, according to how we have been taught or allowed to share our feelings. As contrasting as this season's colors, so too is our understanding of loss, of life and of letting go.

Flocks of birds soar like boomerangs bending south, pledging to return when Winter wears out its welcome. Their promised "Hellos" ease the sadness from their "Farewells" in flight. Departures are difficult. In the face of fleeting permanence we hunger for soil that is solid and for those who will remember and return. Continually, Mother Earth calls us to scatter love with a lavish hand and take love's harvest for granted. Autumn invites us to trust Mother Earth's fruitful presence, especially when the harvest appears barren.

Rollicking raccoons tumble in leaf piles, playing long into the evening and fattening up for the cold season ahead. This is a time to play as well as to prepare. Responding to rigorous responsibilities, requires occasional, refreshing, letting go. Otherwise, one becomes bound in the stiff, gray armor of routine with little room for laughter or for joy.

Growth and healing do not thrive in rigidity. Risking to reveal some insecurities may initiate nurturing connec- tions. Sharing tears and laughter can diminish isolation, and magnify our courage to move forward. Rebraiding snarled memories and releasing fists of anger are means of letting go that foster growth.

When we are no longer shackled with negativity, we can flow in a wave-like rhythm of the squirrel's tail and body.

These free spirited creatures remind us to release from rigid righteousness and relish simple joys. It would be a great loss to miss the fluttering farewell of the monarchs and the playful, warty wink of the toad.

My Friend, the past is always with us and hounds to be befriended. Memories are cruel as well as kind. Typically, we forget things either too insignificant to recall or the memories too pain-full to remember. In their scurrying preparations for Winter, the squirrels challenge us to find a healthy balance between forgiving ourselves when we cannot remember unimportant, minor things and when we have fearfully concealed matters that need tending. In time, significant things inevitably surface. Even forgotten acorns eventually sprout in the most surprising places. In time truth, like seeds, reveals its undeniable presence.

Letting go requires fearing less and risking more. It calls for a delicate balance between laughter and tears, anger and forgiveness. Those who nimbly scamper along the limb of life must learn to be acrobats and sometimes clowns who can recover and grow through slips and falls. For a world with no humor is a bird with no song. A life with no tears is a tree with no leaves. A creature with no anger is a leaf with no veins. A heart with no forgiveness is a flower with no scent on the heel that has crushed it. This is Autumn, The Season of Letting Go and of Growth.

Wrapped in frozen stillness we learned that Winter is the Season of Patience and of Growth. It is a time to learn that we must not force what is not ready to be known or to become. Waiting is a law of life, a measure of love and a test of character. If we fail to learn patience we may rob others of the time they need to grow. A butterfly forced from its cocoon by the breath of warm sighs may die in cold hands that impose on its time.

Growth takes time. Patience is most trying when we see no signs of change. Growth cycles like the seasons, uniquely for each being. Though we cannot always easily see it, growth often occurs beneath the surface. Hidden from the eye during dormant times, seeds that slumber still breathe and grow. Waiting in the darkness, Mother Earth's persistent presence sustains a belief in Spring.

Winter will not be hurried. It forces us to wait. It is the fertile ground for faith to flourish but often exposes its absence. Standing still strains every fiber of our being. We are restless with restrain and awkward with silence. Our impatience increases when answers are withheld, plans are postponed and decisions are delayed. This season most humbles those who believe life is subordinate to them. Mother Earth is a patient teacher.

Winter requires us to live the questions that eventually we must grow into answering. It reveals that patience is not passive. It is the rawest form of courage. It is easier to flee into frenzied activity than stand still in the face of harsh winds that need facing. It is more comfortable to hide in noisy distractions than hear the echoes deep inside that howl for our attention.

Growing through Winter we learn that it takes hope to watch in darkness and believe the night will pass. It takes faith to reach for the sun's return when clouds conceal its presence. It takes courage to risk, to love and believe that life will be renewed. Yet, what would we be without each of these? We must grow through the Winter to celebrate Spring.

Wintry winds whistle for our attention. Strong gusts whisk our imagination. They beckon our Forever Child to joyfully dance with the showering snowflakes. They tinkle the icicles like long slender wind chimes.

Gracefully, fat, fluffy cotton balls fall from the heavens. They transform the forest into a fairyland that glistens with magic. Heavy white blankets drape our tired bending branches. Like robes of royalty they are proudly worn. Eventually we find we can bear more weight than we imagined and stand with self respect in the shadow of the moon.

We hear the cardinals calls more clearly in the cold. Their bright red wings are more visible against the backdrop of still, snowy hillsides. Winter calls us to cherish more what we "say" we treasure and to truly "see" what we fail to notice. Squirrels sliding on the stream's frozen surface brighten the landscape with laughter . . . without which we only survive . . . but we do not fully live.

It takes strength as well as courage to stand still in Winter's cold. Wrapped in chilling darkness, shadowed figures may appear. The ghosts of fear within us, howl the loudest in the night. Hidden secrets sometimes surface when silence is prolonged. Disrobed of denial, Winter prompts us to tend to our wounds. It calls us to name those who carved their initials in our bark, those who splintered our limbs to build fires to warm themselves. Winter patiently longs for us to discover that neither piercing knives or abandoning betrayal can penetrate our shielded, sacred soul. Winter's winds whisper, "Take Back Your Power!"

In the dead of Winter, Mother Earth continues to comfort. She nurtures us with the sap of life that silently flows through our center. Faithfully, She reaches for us with warm rays of sunlight that cut through the cold. Gently, She strokes our furrowed brows and melts our frozen tears. She is one who keeps Her promises. In the chill of night She speaks our name and She calls us each to

remember . . . "Though boundaries may be broken, your sacred spirit remains intact. See harsh times as unfair prunings that still can bring forth life. Be patient, be kind, trust and believe. I will NEVER forsake you."

My Friend, lessons lived surpass knowledge simply learned. Lessons learned "by heart" nourish growth in depth. When we choose to grow through Winter, we discover the magnificence of memory that can heal and can be healed. We learn that memories can bring us roses in December. We find our past can be imprisoning or empowering. Blossoming seeds of insight may be sown in the coldest, darkest nights.

Winter tests the depths of our patience. Can we believe in slumbering seeds beneath the snow-covered ground? Gradually, maturing through Winter, we gain an appreciation of the fortitude required to live the truth-full whole of life. Wise are those who remember the words of the caterpillar, "If you make time to wait on time, time will tell what is true."

Growing through harsh snowstorms, we discover that no distance, no harsh prunings, nor "presumed unending" Winter can withhold the invincible promise of Spring. Life lives on and so do we, far surpassing the limits of frost lines. This is just one of the gifts of insight received from, Winter, The Season of Patience and of Growth.

SECTION II

A REWOVEN PATTERN

My Friend, the seasons of life weave a pattern. When I last wrote to you in, *Grow Deep, Not Just Tall,* I understood each season as I have just shared with you. Life has changed since then and so have we. One is never the same following stormy times. Relationships change too. New patterns appear, woven by the choices that we make.

Do you remember my last words to you before we parted? They were these, "There is no distance or measure of time that can separate the freeing bond of love." Oh, how I missed you and longed for your return, My Friend. Yet how well I have learned that life offers few guarantees beyond the constancy of change and the opportunities for growth.

Of course, we were always a part of one another, My Friend. When my eyes could not touch you, my heart embraced you. Ones we have loved are not replaced by new loves. Nor does the cooling of love's warmth, miles, time or even death, diminish all our memories. Our histories connect us, and our past is always with us. An image and a moment can live eternally in the soul.

Rich, vivid memories brought to life your arms wrapped around me and your soft cheek against my side. Recalling savored moments, I could taste the scent of your

presence. I could feel your sensitive fingers delicately tracing the grooves in my bark. I slept beneath a blanket of warm memories and awakened with tender thoughts of you. Every Spring I hoped and even hungered for a new beginning in our friendship.

In the shroud of foggy days and so many dreary nights, I strained achingly to hear you call for me, to feel you say my name. There were times when I wondered if only in my thoughts would I touch you again. Often I questioned if I ever felt as secure as I imagined in your embrace. Had my loneliness magnified my memory of momentary, mutual, completeness?

I longed for those cherished times we shared, etching treasured images for these times of separation. We were wise to tuck them away. Vividly I imagined your delighted laughter in discovering hundreds of yellow ribbons, each delicately tied to every stem of every one of my beckoning leaves, each with your name, written with the whisper of the breeze.

I hummed melodies of songs we once sang in harmony, dancing as one with the rhythms of the wind. I have no words to express my joy in anticipating, hoping, you would choose to come home to one who freeingly loves you. But . . . you did not. What did come to me was overwhelming, unfair, CHANGE.

Oh, My Friend, Winter was a bitter season that I feared would never end. Ravaging ice storms thrashed me from side to side, tearing my oldest branch from the heart of my trunk. Over many years this rugged branch had become worn and withered. Nonetheless, I was not ready to release this integral part of me. Rarely is the letting go of pieces of ourselves an easy, unemotional task.

Finally the old branch snapped after a long and valiant fight with The Night Winds. Relentlessly it lingered as did my hopes for dreams unseen. Only a few splinters connected us as breaths became more labored. Tenaciously it fought to hold on as it had successfully done so many other seasons. How fiercely I fought to hold it to me, believing it might still blossom as I believed it could.

Impotently watching it gradually slip away, the implications of the practice of patience nearly overwhelmed me. I began to see there might be limits to patience's productiveness but that the fruits of love outlast measured fairness. I had waited a lifetime for the old branch to flower, hoping it would share its fragrance with the forest . . . and just one time with me. However, it blossomed rarely and only when the winds carried its scent away from me.

No amount of patience on my part had brought its scent my way. No other touch could duplicate the one it never gave.

A lifetime of waiting had not been rewarded and time for the old branch was fading. A deluge of questions washed over me. Had my patience been overextended? Had it bound me to fantasies that never could come true? Had my expectations surpassed what the old branch could give and if not, what did that say of me . . . and of the branch that would not bend? If my love was to be fruitful how could I make our parting peace-full and my farewell forgiving?

Choked with throbbing feelings, I stood frozen in the face of our final farewell. A rush of anger unleashed burning tears and a flood of images flashed of all we had not shared, of all it had withheld. It had been such an absent part of my life. Now in its leaving we were both losing what we never had and would never know. Only hushed cries murmured what I tried for years to express. Hesitantly, I reached one last time for the old branch, not in hopes of its reaching back, but to offer a freeing sign of forgiveness for all we never knew.

Finally it fell in silence at the base of my snow-covered roots. I wanted to embrace it one last time but it never reached back for me. Its time had past. So had ours. We parted without words, without an embrace but with quiet and shared understandings. Our last, "Good-bye," had been practiced so many times but accepting its finality

has been awesomely more wrenching than I once believed bearable.

The winds whisked its lifeless form away in the night and it skidded atop the frozen stream. Its departure left me with a hollow in my core but the force of The Night Winds could not topple me. My oldest branch was gone and my trunk was torn but my faith in life persevered. I had given the old branch too much of my power. Now in its absence, I had to be stronger if I was to grow through its leaving. Besides, I had other branches that needed my attention and that I hoped would also tend me. The longest nights of Winter awaited each of us.

Icicles hung from my limbs like long slender tears. I feared I would break beneath the weight of my sadness. Angrily I resented Winter's promise, "The dawn will come," for it was MUCH delayed. There were nights when my only hope was . . . that the morning would NOT find me. Snared by my sorrow, I was beyond consolation.

One early hour at daybreak a noise in the distance diverted my attention. I could hear the crunch of snow as footsteps cautiously neared. A doe timidly approached me. Initially it seemed as hesitant as I to make even a casual connection. Patiently we accustomed ourselves to the presence of one another and gradually grew in guarded trust. The deer was kind and listened well.

I risked to share some pieces of my pain. The gentle presence of the deer soothed some of the sharp edges of my
sorrow. Standing together through Winter's cold, the deer
and I grew in gratefulness for the gift of new found friendship. We were not all alone in the cold.

Spring, like most dawns that year, seemed to have lost its
way into my wintry world. During the day I shivered and at
night I cried. Chilling loneliness like a persistent draft
defied the warmth of Spring. Grieving is hard and lonely
work. Reacquainting with a changed world is frightening.
Even gentle breezes startled me. I feared the force they
might impose. Were they really just the beginnings of more
Night Winds that would lash and take more from me? Had
I been foolish to trust the timid deer? Could its friendship
weather windy seasons or would it too be blown away?

Melodies that once brought joy, now triggered only tears.
My memory failed me. Repeatedly I glanced to my side,
hoping I would see that strong branch still with me. Unwill-
ingly, I played tricks with my mind. It was as though if I
looked quickly, without thinking, I could recapture its presence and not have to accept this awful separation. However, it was gone! Oh, My Friend, it took a long, long time
for my heart to accept what my head knew was true.

My other branches and I talked of the days when we
were all one. It was bonding to share our loss. Yet, it was

isolating as well, for we held unique and sometimes conflicting images of the old branch. We each remembered and grieved very differently. Nonetheless, it was important for us to share our favorite memories and to hear those of our forest friends and family. We did not want to forget or have others not remember. Together we laughed and cried and tried to grow through Spring.

Strange as it may sound, My Friend, remembering to breathe was a chore. I searched for a way to salve the pain but I could not find the secret balm. My soul ached with every breath yet my broken heart kept beating. Life became a lonely battle simply to survive. Even those I thought knew me, seemed so quickly to forget the loss and emptiness that filled my every moment. Those closest to me often felt the farthest away.

My world had stopped but Spring relentlessly continued to unfold. How could things just go on and others be so unaware and unchanged! I had no more predictable, daily routines. Each day and every hour had a huge piece of me that was missing. I was at the mercy of emotions that swept over me with no warning. My world was upended! It wasn't fair! Some mornings I detested the dawn and the notes of songbirds that summoned the sun. Life was calling me to go on but how could I? The thought of my tiny buds unfolding terrified me. I felt in control of precious little.

Deeply rooted beliefs were all shaken. A sense of security eluded me. If such a nightmare could come true last Winter was it safe to hope and dream again? Would I ever know rest-full sleep, without the intrusion of pain-full images, awakening an awareness of a world forever changed? Could I dare risk opening to a new season? Last Spring I believed such ice storms happened only to others. Having been forced to say, "Good-bye," could I bear another, "Hello?" Oh, My Friend, I did grow more patient that long, cold Winter. I also grew more weary in my growing.

I see now I might not have survived, had not Mother Earth kept Her word. Every morning She folded the night back and tenderly placed Her cheek against mine, awakening me with gentle light that softened the dark gloom of depression. Faithfully, She reached for me with soft rays of sunlight and tenderly wrapped me in Her warmth. When I wept She cried with me and rocked me with soothing breezes. Repeatedly She spoke my name. Gracefully She ungloved my bony branches from the ice that held them stiff. Ever so slightly, I began to sense my sap begin to flow through the center of my core. Occasionally the deer would come near and I wondered if Mother Earth had sent her.

Gradually, I noticed that the frozen stream beside me was changing. The solid sheet of ice that had bound her

shore to shore, was cracking and dividing into jagged, jigsaw pieces. They looked so similar to how I felt inside . . . an island severed from the mainland . . . separated, broken and alone.

One morning I saw a blackbird gliding along on one of the floating chunks in the stream. I thought how similar to denial was that jagged piece of ice, carrying one along on the river of grief. Trembling with sadness, I tried to comprehend the magnitude of this irreversible change, this loss of such a part of me and the meaning of the blackbird. It was too painful a perception to acknowledge all at once. I needed pieces of denial to protect me from the cold waters of grief and the frightening waves of reality that washed over me. How could I venture into another season, unaccompanied as in the past? Winter's winds had left me torn and splintered with undefined, new boundaries.

I could not even image myself. What would I see as my new reflection when the stream was free of those frozen islands that cluttered her icy water? Who had I become? Who was I to be? I shivered at the chilling thought that more changes still might come. Where would I find the strength, the desire to move forward? Was this lonely blackbird perhaps a sign, a spirit, a symbol of hope?

Cautiously, I stepped into one day . . . and then one more. Nervously, I welcomed the nose-twitching rabbits that timidly hopped toward me. Together we watched Winter's brown turn to green and found comfort in the knowledge that we were not alone. Dry brittle leaves that had held fast through the cold finally gave way to Spring breezes. Some of the weathered warriors of Winter landed in the stream. I hoped that she would kindly carry them as she had done in seasons past. Others pin-wheeled in the wind, tickling the rabbits' ears as they nibbled on the tender, new, green blades of grass.

Whispering in the night, I tried to calm my sobs with these words, "Surely, no more harm could possibly come to me. Surely, warmer days will bring strength and renew my faith in tomorrow. Oh, Mother Earth, help me find some meaning in all of this, some hope to pull me forward."

Winter finally withered away and Spring began to burst with blossoms. Unscented wildflowers danced all around me in time with the chorus of young frogs. But-terflies fluttered their colorful wings and graceful grasses waved to the clouds. The raccoons' pink tongues lapped in the sunshine as they yawned and stretched in its warmth. The evergreens reached taller toward the heavens and showered their scent on the rebirthing forest. The stream began babbling invitations to be refreshed and the squirrels again played tag.

Spring was bursting forth with new life everywhere. Yet, the wound of grief still ached inside me. Life had changed and so had I. That Spring marked the beginning of life lived daily in the face of unhealed loss. The Night Winds of Winter had refocused my perceptions and redirected my attention. I was more aware of the shattering of the seeds that Spring, than of the new flowers that they fostered.

Time passed and the sun slipped more slowly beneath the warmed horizon. In the light of Summer's longer days I struggled to find some signs or symbols to redirect my course. A company of ants caught my eye as they busied themselves at the base of my trunk. Collectively, they built a mound and tunneled beyond my vision. Some hoisted loads that far out-weighed them. I marveled at their strength and wondered where it came from. I wanted to believe I too could carry the weight of my over-burdened grief and that somehow I too would be strengthened.

I longed to believe . . . that I belonged . . . and to feel at home in my changed and frightening world. I so wanted to believe that Summer would be, "The Season of Fullness and of Growth," the blossoming of Spring's new beginnings. Well, Summer was full indeed, but NOT with what I ever would have chosen. My Friend, I barely survived that Summer . . . FILLED . . . with so many . . . more . . . losses!

A sudden, shearing storm brought a shrieking scream of terror to a hot August sunset. Unbelievably, a second, precious branch of mine was brutally destroyed. This most integral part of me was dashed and then blown away into countless, indistinguishable pieces. It was a horror of horrors for which no soul could prepare.

There was no warning for this last, "Good-bye." I never saw this branch fall, never heard it call for me. I only felt and continue to feel the gnawing ache of cruel uprootedness. Looking back, I remember how it tried to speak to me one last time, to prepare me for a departure it sensed but could not understand. However, the message was too painful to bear, having only just begun to mend from the lashing of Winter's winds. Only now am I beginning to see how important it is, and sometimes critical, to listen care–fully to what others pain–fully try to comprehend and to share.

This precious part of me blew away as ashes fly from burning logs. Battered and torn I stood alone, experiencing fuller meanings to those words than I could ever have fathomed. "Orphaned," was a word I had often spoken, but in one moment, I became. The sorrow-full reality of that word and its isolating implications were immense. The wearing of new terms to define one's self can be staggering. Oh, My Friend, the letting go of my Autumn leaves in earlier seasons only hinted of the abandoned loss I came to know last Summer.

I was more than broken. I was crushed with sorrow. I felt like splintered kindling wood held together by piercing, rusted, barbed wire. Deep inside I was shattered like fine crystal. The pieces tinkled as they fell, and I marveled that no one could hear . . . and that I could no further signal my pain.

A flood of tears and wrenching sobs struggled to give grief a voice. With anger and disbelief I raged, "This cannot be! This is not real! This cannot be happening again! I have only just begun to see what The Night Winds of Winter have done to me. Not again! Not again! Life, you have utterly betrayed me!!!"

Then as suddenly as the storms had flashed, the flames of protest ceased. Instinctively, I pulled my withered limbs into my trunk. Trembling, I crouched close to the ground. Wrapping myself in myself, I sobbed unconsolably, but my limbs could not reach fully around me, and my cries could not relieve the anguish of my shattering sorrow.

Trying to glimpse the magnitude to such a nightmare come true I wept, "Oh Mother Earth, Mother Earth, hold me tight. Cradle me close lest I fall again. There is no safe place in this world for me. Even the cord branch that connected me to the roots of my beginnings has been severed, and I am so alone. Please, hold me, hold me, hold me. Say my name and hold me!"

Reason failed me then and still does. Life is so much more than questions and answers, thinking and logic. How can one reckon any sense to such unreasonable realities? I refused to believe an unseen hand destined such cruel violence. Yet, I could not feel a soothing touch to quiet the gnawing question, "WHY?" I felt only chilling emptiness and raw, isolating loneliness.

Haunting images flashed before me, especially when my eyes closed and I was trapped in my thoughts deep inside. I was lost in a forest overwhelmingly changed. I wandered aimlessly, searching for solace, but my mind came too. Thoughts hounded me with images I feared would never fade. There was no rest for my soul or peace in my mind.

Then one night I fell into a deep, exhausted sleep. In a dream, I heard the voice of a mentor from my youth. It was the wise and wide-eyed owl who did not fear the darkness. Softly he spoke to me, "There is not always justice, only love." In that single, fleeting moment, I felt safe.

Suddenly, the howl of the wind awakened me. Startled and confused, I wondered if this was just a dream or was it "something more." Restlessly, I repeated the owl's words in my mind, "There is not always justice, only love." It seemed so real! Yet, I questioned the meaning of

this message. I wondered, "What comfort are words to a broken heart? What hope is there for faith betrayed?" At long last that night passed . . . but the memory of the owl's message lingered.

Daily the sun rose though often it was hidden by the clouds or swollen eyes. Breezes cooled. I stood limp, unable to fathom the season soon to come, Autumn, The Season of Letting Go and of Growth. Timidly I leaned when the deer came near. Its eyes were kind and its coat was soft. I was never sure just when it would arrive or how long it would stay. However, our brief times together were a comfort. I sensed that someone cared.

My Friend, it was nearly unbearable when the deer I had fearfully trusted, suddenly bolted away. I ached for its return and doubted I would ever risk to share my tears and fears again. Its departure made me question even more, "Was the owl just a dream? Is there love that can be trusted? How will I ever survive . . . and do I even want to?"

More piercing than sticks and stones was the fury of words hurled my way. Responding kindly to insensitive remarks became increasingly difficult and draining. The trite expressions of the pampered pines sizzled like stagnant pond water on the smoldering coals inside me. How dare they believe they understood my splintered world! They were untouched by the storms. Their boughs were intact

and their roots untested. Knotted inside, I stood mute, unable to shield myself from their piercing advice and their cold, empty answers. A mist of anger steamed inside me.

How could others possibly say they knew exactly what I was feeling, when I myself did not know! How dare they urge me to "count my blessings" or deny my anger. Did they not know that death always comes too soon when it takes away someone we love . . . and that loss lingers when love has not yet found its full expression? I did not want the pines to reason my loss or to "fix" my brokenness. Most of all I wanted them to listen and to stay close beside me.

In lonely solitude I wondered if perhaps listening to my pain threatened to unleash tears my "comforters" had long tucked away. Did my presence put them in touch with their own unfinished business and angry pieces they feared to acknowledge? Were their efforts to dry my tears attempts to conceal their secret sobs? Perhaps they spoke their hollow words, attempting to fill the void of screaming silence that shrieked inside of their own frightened souls.

I had too many questions and few "comforting" answers. My energy was exhausted and my patience was worn thin. I viewed life through the lens of overwhelming loss. Everything seemed to reinforce my separateness. Even innocent, minor things magnified my isolation.

I felt estranged from the self I had known myself to be. I was experiencing thoughts and feelings I had not known before the storms. I was edgy and irritable even with those I cherished. One noon my unresolved anger unfairly lashed, "How could you field mice spread picnics in my shades! How dare you celebrate reunions in the shadow of my sorrow!"

The salty taste of my own tears brought me to my senses. Through a veil of humbling embarrassment, I acknowledged a broader perspective. "Why should the field mice be denied their joy just because my heart is broken! The laughter of this world does not cease when some hearts are sad any more than do all tears disappear when some souls are happy."

No, My Friend, there were no simple solutions or quick answers then . . . or now. Nothing and no one could fill the void of such profound loss. Also, there were no safe or healthy ways to avoid those frightening feelings and those haunting, black, night terrors. Gradually, I had to move through them all . . . one . . . by . . . one.

I know now I would not have survived had not Mother Earth nestled me close to Her breast and had I not risked to stay connected with Believers in Life. Those faithful ones could live with the unanswered questions and walk with me through the darkness. They were patient with my impatience. They held me when I could not stand. They

encouraged me to tell my story again and again. They listened, for they knew that through the repeated voicing of my story, I was making real what I did not want to believe but what was unbelievably true. Integrating my past with my present would then free me to move forward with hope. When I could not hear Mother Earth, they were Her voice whispering, "This too shall pass. The night will fade and you will grow through loss. We are here beside you through it all."

My Friend, many seasons have come and gone between then and now and between you and me. Many choices have been made. New perceptions have appeared. I have grappled to find meaning in this awe-full unfairness and have not always been successful. I have struggled to grow through my pain and avoid the risk of being frozen in my sorrow. I am now a Very Changed Tree.

Time has restored me with a healed appearance and profoundly transformed perspective. Though my two beloved branches are no longer visible to you, they remain a present and eternal part of me. I have had to rediscover a new image of myself and of my invisible branches in reshaped connections with me. Also, I have had to grow into new relationships with my remaining branches who are very important to me. We have all coped differently and each has gained new perceptions of ourselves, of each other, and of the meanings of the winds in our lives.

My Friend, it is still unsettling for me when storms return, stirring frightening images. It is poignant when painful dates recycle on the calendar. Some nights when the winds howl, haunting memories sweep over me and I tremble with tears and loneliness. At times, slivers of unforgiveness and left-over anger scratch the new lens I strain to see through. Sometimes I feel as though I have only just begun the journey towards healing. Nonetheless, I am continuing to grow and to discover the "gifts of the lightning," the sacredness of my soul and the power of truth and of love.

My Friend, I have even fewer answers now than when we were last together. I have little advice. I would rather listen, learn, and grow with you. Unique and priceless, the lessons I have lived have bent and sometimes broken me. They have also strengthened and empowered me. Now I have more insights, that I would like to share with you, My Friend.

The whole of life has changed for me. I have not sought new landscapes. I have discovered new eyes through which I see. Now I live and love with heightened hopes and with lower expectations. My willingness to trust is fragile but my faith in life and love are firm. What I have to offer you is the worn and weathered gift of A Spirited Tree.

WELCOME HOME, MY SPECIAL FRIEND
I HAVE TRULY MISSED YOU!!!

SECTION III

AUTUMN REUNION

Again it is Autumn, The Season of Letting Go and of Growth. What a surprise that you have chosen this season to return to me, My Friend. Life never ceases to surprise me. I had nearly let go of hoping for your return and amazingly, here you are! Let me feel your sensitive fingers explore the worn and weathered grooves in my bark. Wrap your arms around me. Press your cheek against my trunk. Hear my heart whisper, "Welcome Home." I hope that in the days to come, we will rediscover one another and nourish our continued growth.

My Friend, I have spent many seasons unraveling and unknotting the bent and broken pieces of my past. I have had to learn to trust again and allow the stream to catch my falling leaves. What a loyal friend she has been, quietly reflecting with honesty and calling me kindly to credibility. She has helped me rediscover a mirrored-image of myself as truly lovely, despite my weathered form.

The stream is a faith-full Believer in Life. Boulders once threatened to halt her current, much like the storms that battered me. Nonetheless, she continued to find ways to move around and even through them. Indeed, those boulders have led to the beauty of her contours, the strength of her spirit, the depth of her character. The stream has been my most faithful friend. She has become my mentor.

At first I could barely glimpse my reflection, following those ravaging storms. Gently the stream beckoned me to see my new form without my beloved branches. She gradually nudged me to see that in mourning the loss of each of them, my memory was very selective. At first I typically recycled only savored thoughts. Some were amazingly embellished by the burden of my grief. At times I had only euphoric recall. Often I questioned if I could survive, having lost what I believed I could not live without.

The stream kindly helped me to see that my branches and my relationships with them were never perfect. They never could be. Yet, there is in each of us such a hunger for fairy tale perfection and a longing to avoid shadowed truths. Like all relationships, ours were flawed as we were a blend of imperfect pieces. Eventually I began to see and to accept what was real and true . . . including new perceptions of myself. Over time I learned to release my illusions of make believe and to feel more "at home" in truth-full solitude.

Listen to the stream celebrating your return. Hear her current trickling songs and dancing little ripples in rhythms that rhyme. Look at the chestnut-brown cattails swaying near her bank. They are waving, "Farewell" to Summer and "Welcome Back" to you. My Friend, I hope we can say "Hello" to Autumn and to one another in new ways this season of growth.

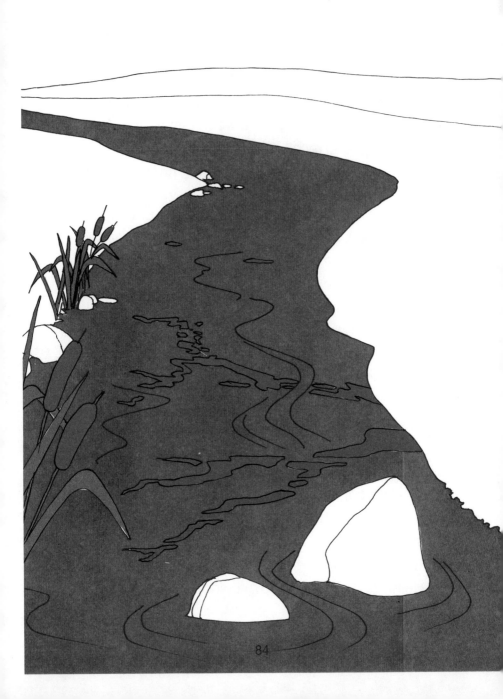

84

The red tongues of the sumac are whispering the onset of fall. It will not be long and my colors will reach their peak again. The shorter days have caused the green shields of my leaves to retract, and my real colors are surfacing. They were always there, only concealed by the sunny, Summer days of lush fullness. Now that the nights are longer and colder, what always has been, is exposed.

Can you see parallels, My Friend, in our relationship and in the relationships you share with others? Our real colors seem to surface when the nights feel like forever and dawn is delayed like an unkept promise. Can you see parallels in yourself? Some of the colors we discover are not admirable. Some may be frightening. Some are utterly astonishing, amazingly affirming. How interesting it is to see which colors we choose to focus upon . . . and to intensify.

Difficult times and unchosen changes can unleash and reveal hidden colors. It is exciting when we realize that as constant as change, so too is our option to choose the shades we display and magnify in our lives. Like a painter with a pallet, we color on the canvas named, "Myself." Like critics of art, we judge others by the colors they display. Too seldom do we recognize that the shapes and colors visible on the canvas only hint at the magic hidden in the Masterpiece.

Hopefully, as we become more seasoned sculptors of life, we realize that seeing is not believing. BELIEVING IS SEEING. Boulders and storms can mean "more" than destruction. It is not "what" happens to us that makes or breaks us. Rather, it is "how we choose to see and to respond to what happens," that marks the differences between victims, survivors and Believers in Life. Acting on the power to CHOOSE, rekindles the spark of hope and life.

My Friend, I believe the wiser we become, the fewer answers we prescribe for others and the more responsibly we sweep in front of our own doorsteps. The deeper we grow the more honestly we examine the perceptions we hold and the choices and the attitudes we choose. Some of the most important considerations for us to examine are these:

- What do we believe about ourselves, our circumstances, and the choices available to us?

- Are we choosing to move beyond victimization and working towards becoming Believers in Life?

- Are we aware that by "growing deep, not just tall," we can bring a brilliance called "compassion" to a world too often dulled by despair and disillusion?

- **OR** . . . do we choose to give our power away, to place our brush in the hands of others and of circumstance, pretending that we have no other options?

My Friend, the choices are ours to freely make and with each one there is a consequence. If we choose to give our brush away, we may become victims of negativity and opt for a world of camouflaged, jaded reality. Trapped in an armor of unrelenting anger and sadness (though "justified" they may be), we sing a litany of victimized misfortune for anyone who will listen.

Some wield swords of anger. They cut others down, trying to even their inherited unfair score. Rehashing their past, they fight to justify their present irresponsibility. Others withdraw into isolating depression. Still others use a variety of substances to anesthetize themselves and choose to live a numbed existence. Some frantically try to silence the voices inside, and the memories that will not die, with constant noise and frenzied activity. Each of these options is an effort to cope, an attempt to deal with pain. Each may result in avoiding a truth that is fearfully, or shamefully hidden. Sadly, each may lead . . . to even greater pain.

My Friend, it does NOT have to be this way. Remember those other choices! It is possible to break through our fears, our tears, our weakness and monotonous routines of habit. By letting go in ways I am just beginning to more fully understand, we can awaken from nightmares and become our dreams. We can become "more" in spite of what threatens only to diminish. We can grow, My Friend, if we COMMIT TO CHANGE!

It is possible to reroot, to risk, to trust and love again. We can take back our brush and learn to paint a powerful, meaning-full masterpiece on even torn and wrinkled canvas. Also, there need be no shame in allowing others, and asking others, to help us grasp our brush again and teach us how to make graceful, colorful strokes. Always the choice is ours!

The most masterful creators I know are those artists whose medium is life itself; life full of unfairness, unchosen seasons and seemingly impossible obstacles. Without hammer, clay or drum, they neither pound nor impose. Their medium is being. Their presence adds beauty to the landscape of life.

In the face of misfortune they refuse to be diminished. In response to unfairness they become MORE . . . not less. Drawing on roots they themselves sometimes question, they continue to hope and to grow. Storms may whittle away their outer attractiveness and exhaust the strength of their spirit. However, over time those same storms only prove to be chisels that chip away at what conceals their raw courage and masks their real beauty.

In response to misfortune they continually find ways to recreate and to celebrate. Whatever their presence touches, increases life. From ashes they fan light alive. Awakening from shattered dreams they envision new

horizons. In the silence of despair they hum soothing melodies. Washed anew and refreshed in their own fallen tears, they become wells of compassion for others.

These masterful creators weave memories, paint visions, and sculpt beauty out of brokenness. They sing, laugh, love and cry. They work through their anger and learn to forgive. They listen to our Mother Earth and search to find their siblings. Creatively and courageously they risk to become who life challenges them to be. They are the artists of being alive, living treasures, true Believers in Life. Oh, My Friend, I question if I would have seen this day, had not those creative examples helped me find my way. What gifts are my sisters and brothers!

Now it is Autumn once again, but what a changed season it is. I had nearly lost hope for your return, My Friend, and to my joy-full surprise, here you are! More than ever before, I realize that life truly is playing hide-and-seek everywhere we turn.

In the days and seasons ahead, let us continue to help one another let go of our illusions and discover more and more how we each can become . . . genuine masterpieces, pieces of the Master of Mystery that sparks life alive in all of us.

The forest is a blaze of color. Glistening reds, oranges, yellows and scarlets shimmer in the sunlight. The wind restlessly rustles all it touches as if to nudge us to notice this fleeting hour. It will not last. Like all things and like all those we treasure, it too is on loan and for such a little time.

I wonder what you see in this moment, My Friend. I used to believe I knew without asking. Now I wonder how well I really knew you and how much I simply assumed. We live with so many illusions. We act on so many assumptions. It is no wonder we have so many conflicts!

Often we assume that others see or "should" see the same colors that we do. To minimize misunderstandings we must cautiously clarify our perceptions and concede that we see through different lenses. Both the eagle and the ant see their "real" forest.

We each discover truth in our own time. We bring our truths and less-than-total vision to each moment. Our yesterdays color the climate of today. Why do we repeatedly try to force "our truths" on others? Insights come from the inside. They cannot be imposed from the outside. Why is it so hard for us to agree to disagree respectfully? We cannot spin the dials of cycled seasons.

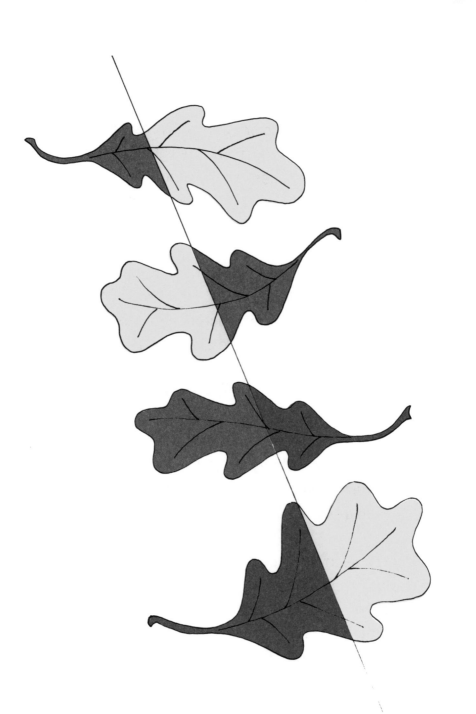

Oaks, maples, willows and pines, we all live September uniquely. "The glory of this season is a harmony in contrasts." It sounds like a contradiction. It is and yet it is not. It is like the whole of life, full of losses and of gains, of greetings and good-byes and of complimenting opposites that blend. This Autumn is similar and yet unlike any other. It is like you and me, My Friend.

We are absolutely unique and simultaneously we are more alike than we are different. What is most intimate and personal is also most universal. We all hunger to love and to be loved, to be meaning-fully connected. We all want to matter in our world, to be chosen, to be remembered. How we see and satisfy these same hungers is what separates and sometimes incites us to anger and aggression. Perplexingly profound yet simply stated, life is a paradox and each of us is a precious-paradox-personified.

Making a relationship work is like two porcupines trying to find warmth by curling up with one another on a chilly Autumn night. Each has different lengths of quills that raise or relax based on safety and trust. Each seeks the warmth the other has to offer. Finding just the right way to get close without piercing one another is a delicate quest for balance. Just when they think they have it "right," one may suddenly turn in their sleep or one quill may grow or retract.

Maintaining long lasting warmth in any relationship takes effort, commitment and risk. Reciprocal love is impossible without mutual vulnerability. Loving relationships are filled with reaching out and withdrawing, giving and receiving. Such "harmonies in contrast" demand the whole of who we are and challenge us to become all that we can be. A relationship For-All-Seasons is a rare and precious gift.

Love fuels life alive. Without love, life is barren. Love is to life as the sun is to seasons. Both the sun and love reveal themselves with differing intensities, in different seasons of our lives. Both can nurture tiny seeds or quell them through denial. Both can blossom buds to life or harm them with over-exposure. Like lost acorns and fisted buds, we long to be discovered and to blossom in glowing warmth. Too little can stifle growth's potential. Too much can consume, exhaust or destroy.

Life with no passion is a fire with no flame. The thrill and excitement of love ablaze fills us with energy and heated desires. Inevitably, raging flames calm and cool. Radiance looms, as embers glow, drawing us to warming companionship. A breeze can fuel the flames again and fill us with fiery feelings. However, as Life is Change and Growth is Optional, so too, love changes as relationships grow. Each must define what is desired, expected and offered. How much do we choose to give or demand to fuel our love alive?

A blazing fire is spectacular and hot, thrilling, exciting and sensual. However, standing too close, too long to the flames can singe, blister or scar us. Remember, we touch the ultimate only temporarily. As we hunger for love, life longs for balance. Standing too far from love's fire can chill the soul and freeze our feelings, hopes and desires. Love's flame needs respect-full tempering and faith-full tending. Each must breathe on flickering coals or they die in the cold, dreary, damp of indifference.

My Friend, will you make a contract of trust with me? It will be a blueprint for building a sound foundation, a rekindling of friendship's flame. It will be a guide to help us grow through each of the seasons to come:

- First, let's each promise to look within ourselves and attend to those quills that need tending and mending.
- Second, let's promise to honestly risk asking for what we need with the acceptance that each will occasionally make mistakes and that neither is expected to fill the emptiness of the other.
- Third, let's affirm one another kindly in ways that do not smother or burn.
- Finally, let's be open to helping each other grow through changing times and find new ways to support, to celebrate, to play and to say, "I love you."

From this day on, when one of us hurts the other, let's try to remember the words of the spider who long ago

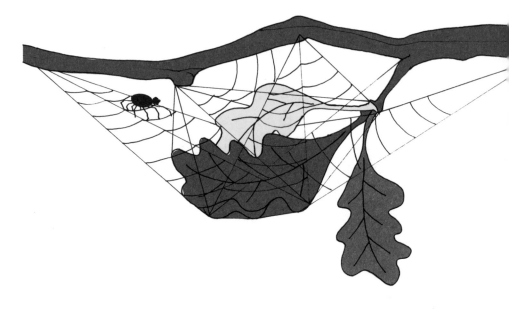

wisely advised me. He said, "When someone hurts or rejects you, it typically is not with deliberate intent, although there are certainly exceptions! More often than not, that individual is trying to get needs met, to warm or to shield themselves. Sometimes you are injured in their process. Remember, the acorns you drop to reseed the forest may spell disaster for the unsuspecting crickets singing in your shade."

I must tell you, My Friend, when you did not return to me when I was struck by storms, I questioned if you cared. I thought for sure you must have known how much I needed you. When I could not find a way to tell you so myself, I assumed another would inform you. Seasons passed and my angry silence simmered. I wondered if and when you ever would return and how I would respond. Now I see why you never came. Unlike the deer who knew and chose to run away, you never even knew. Forgive me, Friend, for I misjudged you.

My Friend, there is no One True Way to see or to be. There is no Single Right Way to show love or to speak love's language. If we, like Autumn, hope to live as "harmonies in contrast" we must let go of narrow perceptions and openly discover truth revealed in differing hues. We must hear love spoken with different accents. We must make time to clarify our expressions and learn from both the eagle and the ant.

Be aware, My Friend, even in relationships grounded in truth and love, conflicts remain inevitable. Resolutions can be reached only when both hearts and heads hear openly and speak honestly. Trust grows where truth lives. When games begin, trust unravels. Love focuses on truth for there it sees itself. When truth calls, we must sometimes respond with heartfelt, "I am sorry. I was wrong."

Remember too, My Friend, silence is NOT always golden like the harvest moon of Autumn. There are times when it is ugly, destructive, divisive and cruel. Actions DO speak louder than words, revealing what we hold in our hearts. So too, words withheld like actions untaken give voice to what is real. Failing to speak in defense of a friend echoes our hollow commitment. Failing to voice feelings that fester and ooze can poison the roots of a friendship. The cutting edge of silent contempt can sever one soul from another.

Silence is NOT the absence of expression. Its pitch can be piercing. Its echoes linger and lengthen with time. Unspoken needs, hurts and desires can injure, isolate and destroy. Words withheld, like affection withdrawn, can be a cold, selfish means to control. Silence may be selected as an icy power-play, an effort to deny behavior. It places others in the position of having to guess where we are, what we want and how we feel. Silence forces others to read our unclear signals. Often we punish others when they guess wrong.

Silence is sometimes a cowardly escape, a ploy to run from conflict or responsibility. Remember, the opposite of love is not hate. It is total, silent indifference. Sealed lips can scream hostile, judgmental rejection. Why some are quick to condemn and selfish with words that are kind, is a sad and serious question to ponder. Wrapped in silence, love does not grow and in time may shrivel and die.

My Friend, there is no more misunderstood silence between us. The quiet we now share is the hushed respect of two who wait patiently to listen for each heart to speak. It is the silence that connects and does not isolate. Reverently standing in the still of the moment, we can feel the power of presence. There are no words to contain the mystery we experience, as clouds create magical formations. In silence we see the spirit in the wind. Yes, the silence we now share is mutually understood, My Friend. It makes room for the sacred unspeakable.

Autumn leaves are falling all around us. We are letting go of misunderstandings that once divided us. Truth is falling into place. Trust is gradually growing. We are beginning again to grow through our friendship. We are harvesting new insights and singing new songs in three-part harmony. I am so happy that you chose to return . . . and amazingly in this season of letting go! My Friend, allow me again to humbly say . . . I am so sorry I unfairly misjudged you.

A rustling choir of colors voice a crescendo of Autumn. I am impatient, at times even irritable, with those who allow these beauty-full days to slip by with no awareness, no acknowledgement. I see you wink at me, My Friend. I feel you gently invite me to remember my early years when I too paid little attention to moments like these. Yes, true friends kindly call us to credibility. And yes, it is probably because I have survived so many bleak and barren times, that I so vehemently embrace this fleeting moment. "The gifts of the lightning" are becoming more clear.

Look, simultaneously without a sound three slender, silky, stems let loose their grasp. Three shiny leaves wave to each other as they spiral down together. Suddenly the air is a swirl of color. Reddish browns twist and twirl like streamers from my highest branches. It is as though rusty rainbows are falling from the heavens, weaving a patch-work quilt of leaves to blanket the cooling forest floor.

Like vivid memories that warm cold and lonely separations, these fallen leaves will nurture and protect my roots. In time they will become part of the soil, for life is never lost. It is only changed. Oh, how many memories I have had to blend into the tapestry of my past. How many losses I have had to learn from and grow through.

My Friend, Autumn's colorful climax radiates through me. I am no longer an observer of this season. I am Autumn. More poignantly than ever, I know the fragility of life. I feel a sense of reverence for all that life makes holy, including the sacredness of you . . . and of me! Now I understand how temporary are these mysterious, magical moments. I realize that happiness is tasted in little bits. It is a gift not a guarantee, a joy to be shared, not a prize to be possessed. What a gift this is, My Friend, to celebrate this season once again together! In this Autumn moment I am truly happy.

Intrinsically I am one with Autumn as I am with each of the four seasons. Yet, ultimately I am alone, even when you are with me. Strange as it may sound, accepting this fact has calmed that gnawing sense of loneliness that never fully fades. Coming to terms with this reality has drawn me to reach beyond what I can touch, to seek for deeper root-ings through The Spirit that breathes through all. Mother Earth alone knows the whole of Her creation. She touches us uniquely through each other in ways that bring forth life, sometimes pain-fully . . . always meaning-fully. Continu-ally, She calls us to reunions with our siblings.

My Friends, I am learning to reroot in a power I believe will not betray me, no matter how harshly The Winds may blow. Beyond description, this Root of roots connects me with the center of all life, to myself, to my world . . . and to you.

As life constantly changes and my soul continues to hunger for stability, I am discovering that this Root of roots is trustworthy and nourishing. Believing in what I cannot fully comprehend, I am discovering this Root relentlessly reaches out for me. I am finding that my heart does know truths perhaps my head can never hold. Truth is expanding.

Perplexing paradoxes are in vivid focus at this point in my life. Strength and vulnerability are my intimate, constant companions. There is no longer a clear cut duality between what is and what is not. Because I have lost so much, vulnerability sweeps over me like a sudden shiver, stirring unsettling thoughts and trembling my leaves. I ache to trust this Root of roots for I am intimately aware I could still and I know in time I will . . . lose . . . again and again.

At the very same time I feel strong, grounded, and secure, comforted in the knowledge I have matured through past stormy seasons. Having grown through it all thus far, I believe I will continue to do so and that I will be strengthened and sustained. I have learned to release illusions of tangible permanence, to wait patiently in the fullness of the moment and to risk beginning again and again. Then suddenly the breeze catches my leaves. It stirs vulnerability and I question if The Cord to Life reaches out for me. Will I have the strength and support to carry me through fear? Will I survive if winds again storm me?

My Friend, the forest has changed significantly since we were last together. Can you see the differences? Some are obvious and many are not. Storms typically take hidden tolls. Visibly, two of my branches were torn from my trunk. Not so apparent are the deep wounds gouged by grief and trust that was betrayed.

Storms strike unfairly and often unreasonably. Though they sliced right through me, they never touched the evergreens. At times I feel lonely, like a tree set apart in the middle of the forest. I wonder why we oaks have been so beaten while others have been spared. Sometimes I feel jealous, angry and afraid. I question, "Is there any justice in the world of broken hearts? What were those words the owl spoke so many seasons past?" Clear vision eludes me when clouded by doubts, fear and pain.

I see the majestic pines standing straight and tall and still intact. Winter only bent a few of their boughs and none were fully broken. Spring and Summer both were kind to the handsome spruce. My Friend, they are even fuller than when you last stood here with me. They all were untouched by the lightning of last August. Most seem to have forgotten the storms that I endured. They seem not to notice profound changes in me. Only a precious few remember my monumental moments that time does not erase. Often I question if there is a "gift" in all that we receive?

Sometimes I wish I were an evergreen! I wonder why we oaks must drop our leaves EVERY year and stand half naked through the Winter. We are even more lonely when the birds hover in the fullness of the evergreens' lush boughs, securing warmth and protection from Winter's windy cold. I miss my fair-feathered friends. Only rarely do they perch on our barren limbs when ice rims our gnarled, naked branches.

I wonder if the evergreens ever envy our colors. I wonder if perhaps they know loss in ways I cannot see and if they ever cry. I wonder if they can feel the fullness of this moment, having only known green in all their seasons. At times I question if our Cords to Life spring from the same soil Source. Life can be so unjust and there are so many things beyond my ability to reason!

My Friend, I wonder if some questions have no answers. I wonder if growth depends on the kinds of questions we ask and continue to recycle. I am discovering that I mull over and over different questions at different times.

In the daylight hours, I usually focus on "How?" How can I grow from here? How can I bring some meaning out of these multiples of losses in my life? How can I manage to hold on until sundown and then wait through the night for the morning? However, in the darkness, when I cannot sleep . . . my heart cries, "Why? Why? Why?"

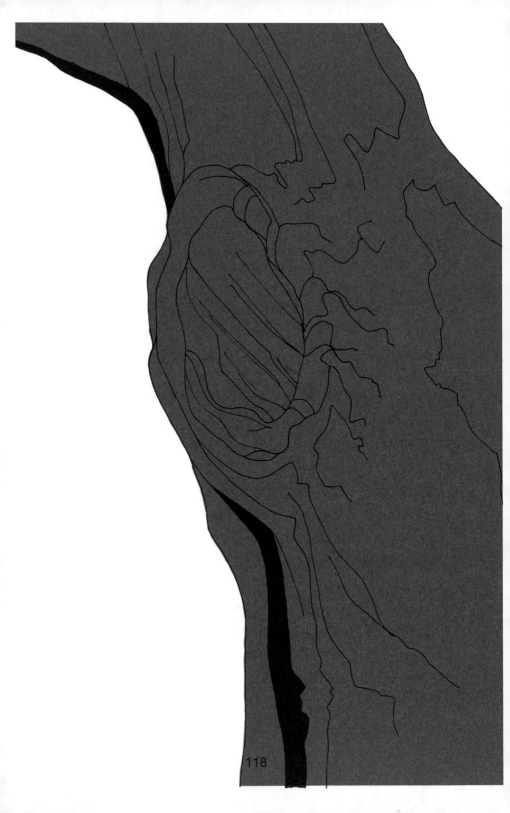

118

Listen, My Friend, my acorns are tapping a farewell rhythm on the rock in the stream beneath my boughs. Only a few weeks ago the red tongues of the sumac whispered the onset of Autumn. Now they have all burst into blazing crimson and the damp, decaying scent of October permeates every breath. Autumn is slowly slipping away.

Sometimes I am amazed that I have survived and truly grown, despite so many farewells. I am amused and somewhat saddened that it takes so long to realize what is most important. Time becomes more precious when there is less of it to waste. Difficult times have taught me that what is most valuable is often hidden from the eye, touched only with the heart and preserved through memory, ritual and symbols.

My Friend, remember, we survivors are always so much more than we appear. TIME DOES NOT HEAL ALL. However, time does help us to gradually mend. It allows us to gain new perspectives. As time passes, our wounds scar over but we are never, EVER, the same. The marks of nightmares come true never fully fade and that is fortunate. It would be very sad to have no painful memories, for the gift of compassion is received and passed on only by broken hearts that remember.

If we allow time to become a trusted companion, we can gradually learn to befriend our shadows and make peace with our pain and sorrow. Why some are more often caught in the storms I cannot explain. However, I DO NOT BELIEVE that The Source of The Wind selects some to be shielded and others to be stormed. Some questions simply have no easy answers! I DO BELIEVE that life breathes through each of us, My Friend, and that our shared and sacred spark is not to be brazenly extinguished or indifferently ignored.

Those of us who have nearly lost our flame are challenged to remember and to reframe our pain. Tears and turmoil can transform the soul in positive life-giving ways. Finding meaning in the hurt-full past may enlighten the future that awaits our choices.

When our spark again glimmers, life calls us to broaden our concerns beyond our own needs, to reach out and respond to our world that weeps for meaning. Ultimately it becomes our privilege to blow care-fully on the faint, flickering embers of those who struggle in the shadows. Life calls us to become wounded comforters in the forest, faith-full tenders of hope's flame, grounded spirits who offer consistently gifts of joy and compassion.

Perhaps the most tragic of all are those who have not grown through their histories, those who choose to recycle

and reimpose demeaning patterns. Having once been the victims, their fists remain clenched with unresolved anger and pain. Once they gain "power," they bitterly become the ones they once feared, the abusers. Similarly, peons become dictators. Patriots become imprisoners. Each has failed to learn what life tried to teach them. Each failed to discover that power that is pure is like strength that is true. Both are life-giving, respect-full and kind.

In order to grow through our histories and to be transformed we must choose to relearn and reroot. My Friend, you may not have noticed but even the structure of my roots has changed since we were last together. Under the surface of the browning grasses that skirt my trunk, sprawls a renewed, restructured root system.

Following Winter's Night Winds and Summer's Wind Shear, I struggled to hold on and I grappled for support. I began to feel that some of my roots were not stabilizing me. Some were siphoning my strength, even poisoning my potential for survival. Hauntingly, I recalled the voices of craggy oaks during my sapling years, rigidly requiring independence and the absolute silencing of any shadowed, fragile feelings. Asking for help and acknowledging fear were strictly forbidden of oaks. With an increasing sense of sadness and of loneliness, I began to see that I needed MORE than my stoic, old oak rules allowed.

At the same time I happily recalled the laughter we shared and the good times we had, celebrating some of our old oak traditions. It was confusing trying to sift through all the shoulds and should nots, the nevers and forevers. It was frustrating trying to find truth in the mire of so many contradicting absolutes. My goal was not to blame or to punish any who falsely informed me. It was to reclaim what was treasurable and to let go of what was not.

Gradually, Winter let loose its frozen grip on the soil and on my soul. The earth began to soften and so did my sorrow. Cautiously I risked to reach deep and deeper still for the Root that most intimately bound me to Mother Earth. Slowly I opened myself to feel the sap of life flow through my core. It was frightening to release from rigid rules and risk to reroot anew. Nonetheless, the dawn arrived every morning and in the night Mother Earth embraced me. Ever so gradually I risked to trust, to believe Her love would ground me. My tap root began to extend.

Slowly I opened my eyes to truths I did not want to see. Gradually I recognized that my fear of the unknown and my anxiety over increasing loneliness, caused me to choose to stay attached to what was harmfully familiar. However, if I chose to grow, I would have to reframe old images and regroove old routines. If I wanted to grow . . . I would have to accept . . . I WOULD HAVE TO CHANGE!

I would have to let go of entanglements with the roots of trees that were not healthy. Sad, but true, that letting go increased the weight of grief. Disengaging from decaying and even strangling connections can strangely leave us feeling suffocated and bereaved by our own hand. Relearning and rerooting is internal civil war. Pieces of us die as other pieces come alive.

Some of those I hoped would support me did not want me to change. They were angry with my efforts, criticized my choices and attempted to intimidate my courage. I was often afraid and sometimes betrayed. At times, My Friend, I still am. Stubbornly I refused to cease trying. I made some mistakes and a few unwise investments, but with each one I learned and I grew. Renewing old routines was the most unsettling for me, for everything was changing and so was I. In the midst of crisis, scripts are unwritten and boundaries are unclear. I needed new maps to find a new way.

Relying only on the past no longer was sufficient. You see, My Friend, I had grown "up" in the shadow of many taller trees who repeated the patterns of the past, typically unquestioning recycling routines. At times I felt myself a traitor to dare challenge The Way Of The Oaks. Often I was criticized for even suggesting another way. It took more courage than I imagined and strength beyond my own to remain committed to *Grow Deep, Not Just Tall.*

One chilly March morning I noticed a blackbird take flight from a lonely chunk of ice, floating in the thawing stream beside me. The breeze sang a long-forgotten melody that quickened my spirits and triggered new thoughts. In that same moment I felt the weight of a robin gently land on my yawning, outstretched limbs. Her voice was soothing. Her words were kind.

The robin reminded me that I had always tried to do what I believed was right. However, some of what I had accepted had never been tested until winds nearly snuffed hope's flame. Some things I needed to reconsider. Some of what I had been taught needed reteaching.

The robin helped me to see that my roots had become an unquestioned network of beliefs. Faced with stormy new realities, it was obvious that my old root system no longer held me safe. Life had changed and I must choose to reroot or not to grow. Gently the robin revealed a freeing and empowering insight:

> What we live ....we learn
> What we learn ....we practice
> What we practice............................we become
> What we become.................has consequences

Previously unaware of unquestioned rootings, I had become what I lived, what I learned and what I practiced. The robin helped me to see I had many more choices. I could learn to reroot. I COULD CHANGE! I could grow far beyond my perceived limitations. I could even do things generations of oaks were never allowed to do. If I searched, I might even rediscover my lost little acorn, my own Forever Child.

Responsive to my tears and the fragile feelings such a thought generated, the robin spoke softly,

"Breathe, frightened tree. You are not as alone as you feel. Be gentle with you. You may not always get what you want, but in time, you will almost always find what you need, if you search and if you ask. I will be your faithful friend, though never perfect. You will meet others too who will nurture you and help you grow. Your "family" is being redefined.

"You CAN learn how to reroot and you WILL discover new strength and courage. The Tap Root to which you are now connecting will faithfully nurture you, even though you cannot see it and sometimes you may doubt its presence. Others may still leave you, break their promises and may even try again to carve their initials in your bark. In the face of such violations and disappointments your Tap Root will sustain you. Far beyond the end of time, YOU will always be with you, connected with your Tap Root.

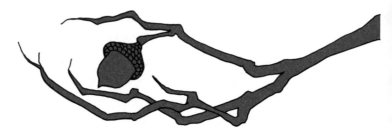

"Spirited Tree, you are now grounding in the realization that YOU are the one you have been searching for. YOU are the one you have been waiting for to come home to you. YOU are one of many, through whom The Spirit speaks. Gradually and tenderly YOU will learn how to hold your abandoned little acorn, your own lost Forever Child, in the safe and loving embrace of your branches."

The wisdom of the robin became a harbinger of surging growth deep within me. Reflecting on earlier days I was surprised I never paid much attention to the robin until after the Winter that nearly broke me. I never really listened to her until after the August that nearly banished my belief in another Spring. Prior to those times, I focused on the brightly colored bluejays and cardinals in the pines. They seemed so bright and more worthy of my attention. Robins seemed so plain, so common. Now memories of times with the robin are priceless and these words from the owl hold new meanings for me, "The eyes of the wise see the miraculous in the common."

My Friend, time is a teacher, an instructor of insight, a sifter of wheat from the chaff. I smile as I recall special times with my favorite oaks who nurtured me the best that they could. Some of what they taught no longer works for me. At the same time, there were many truths tucked in their simple sayings. In my youth the breadth of their vision escaped me. Only recently have I come to value

the wisdom they shared in profound simplicity. How insight-full are those phrases I heard repeatedly:

"You cannot put an old head on young shoulders."
"You always find what you look for."
"Sweep in front of your own doorstep."
"Become the friend you long to find."
"We will cross that bridge when we come to it."
"Do not burn the bridges behind you."
"This too shall pass. Be faith-full."
"Find meaning in all you experience."
"Discover a gift in all you receive."
"Become truly who life calls you to be."
"Let the light within you shine brightly."
"Let go, laugh lots, love lavishly."

I miss my beloved branches and the good times I recall. What they offered that was not treasurable I have learned to release and over time to forgive. Recalling all those who were dear to me is a comforting, poignant reunion of memories. Each had something to teach me. Each held a gift to offer. Now each one lives on in my heart of hearts and through my memories. Remember, My Friend, even death cannot separate loving, true connections. Nor can any distance or measure of time sever the freeing bonds of love.

My Friend, when we are in the midst of unchosen circumstance or gnawing uprootedness, treasured images can help bridge the gaps between savored yesterdays and hoped for tomorrows. Tucked safely in our minds and in our imaginations, treasured memories connect us with special seasons passed and longed for sunrises. These pictures furnish warmly the interiors of our minds and are safe places we can turn to when we are frightened, sad or lonely. Among the most precious gifts we can give today are cherished memories for all the tomorrows yet to come.

My Friend, when I was trapped in the midst of my stormiest seasons, memories of your presence soothed and befriended me. I was swaddled in the feelings they stirred. Now I stand amazed that we are together again listening to my acorns tap a farewell rhythm to Autumn.

Come a little closer now, My Friend. Warm my wrinkled bark with the breath of your sighs. I am imprinting these moments in my memory. With compassion, let us explore the internal landscapes of our most intimate Autumns. May we help each other to mend old hurts and to reroot in healthy soil. Let us help each other hold on to our dreams and to let go of what inhibits birthing life. Oh, My Friend, I am so thank-full that you have chosen to return!

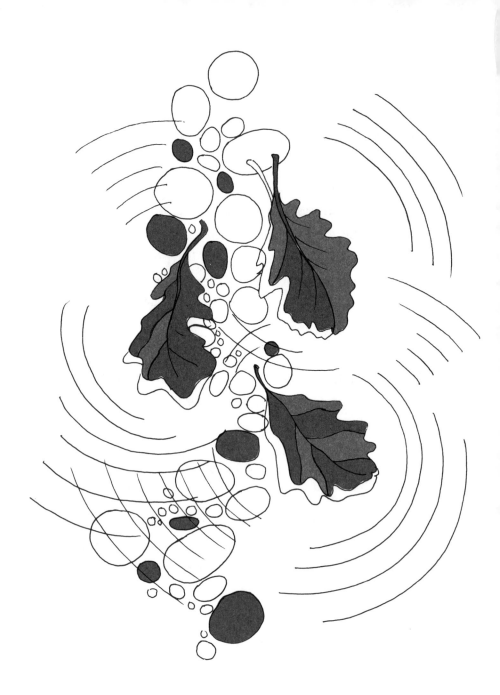

The stream calls reassuring invitations to those linger-
ing, leathery leaves that tenaciously delay their departure. She understands their fearful hesitation to let go.
She knows how hard it is for them to believe that she will
safely carry and not consume them. Beckoning to the
waving branches overhead, she sings:

"I will not take your colors from you. I seek only to
reflect your loveliness. The closer you approach me,
the more vividly you will discover yourselves. I will
openly receive you, embrace you and uphold you.
Then gracefully we will flow downstream together."

My Friend, that was the same song she sang so many
Autumns ago, when you were last here with me. Do you
remember? The stream was trying to teach me about
loving relationships. Trusting was easier then. It is harder
for me now, having known so many losses.

The stream has always been true to her word. Yet, some
of my leaves still fear believing even the faithful stream.
Having known repeated turbulent times has made it
more difficult to believe, even the believable. Restoring
trust that has been broken is no easy task. For some it is
like trying to suck a wave from the sand once it has
washed ashore.

Look, it's a spunky, spotted sandpiper just like the one we saw years ago when you sat here with me. It brings back so many happy thoughts. Look at its spindly little legs dash along the bank. Suddenly it stops. Tilting its head, it is staring at us! I wonder what it is wondering. Does it possibly remember us or do we remind it of others? Perhaps it questions where you have been or how we have reconnected. Maybe it is simply a gift to bring us joy, a trigger to recall past, sunny Autumn days.

My Friend, it is important to remember that the Autumn of today stirs thoughts of previous Autumns that have fallen into history. Subsequent seasons may blur specifics and fade sharp images. Nonetheless, every Autumn is accumulatively marked on the calendar of the soul.

Similarly, one more good-bye may hold magnified significance when added to previous, unprocessed farewells. The weight of one more hurt may be unbearable when added to the burden of too many heartbreaks. One more broken promise or sad disappointment makes trusting that much harder. Each one adds to our accumulated loss and sometimes to a sense of real or imagined victimization.

We all hold visions of how life "should" unfold and what we ought to harvest. However, experiences teach us that life and relationships are not always our dreams come

true. Both can be harshly disappointing. Consequently, the stream sometimes sadly reflects truths we do not want to see, for friendships can bring buzzards as well as sandpipers.

Feelings instinctively mount in response to whatever we experience. Although they are not always expressed or even named, they roll and rumble inside. Anger is an especially challenging emotion. It is critical to understand that it is normal and necessary. Anger is as natural a response to unfairness as is the snap of my limbs when they are broken in the wind.

Anger needs truth-full attention and care-full expression. Rooted in perceived injustice, anger can be triggered by intimidation. Loss of control or an increase in fear also increase the likelihood of its expression. Unharnessed anger can explode into thundering rage, sometimes sadly with violent implications. Once ignited it can billow like a fire gone wild in the wind. A forest can be destroyed by an undetected fire. A forest can be flattened by flames gone wild with rage. A soul can be consumed by an unforgiving spirit. So can we, My Friend!

Anger that is denied crackles and accumulates beneath the surface. Eventually, it may result into depression and withdrawal. Unattended anger does not disappear.

Ignored, it simmers and can be ignited by an innocent, unintended spark of inequity. Then suddenly, blazing emotions burst into expressions of heated rage or over-flow in a torrent of tears. Typically this flashing response is in magnified disproportion to the circumstance. Bewildered observers often mistake the focus of such fury. Yes, feelings like flames can be frightening.

Unprocessed anger weaves a ring of fire. Others may want to come close but they feel the heat and wisely fear risking being blistered. We must reckon with our anger, with our unfinished farewells and the hurts we did not deserve. If we do not, they take a heavy toll over time. They can ruin relationships and eventually consume our capacity to risk and to trust . . . and . . . to love again. Unresolved anger isolates its owners. Butterflies do not fly into thorny, burning bushes.

Anger is energy that summons attention. It does not sim-ply dissipate or evaporate with time. Its effects can be destructive. It can singe tender connections and smother the capacity for intimacy. Allowed to build, the white flame of malice hisses in the darkness, hungering for revenge, scheming for a way to get even. However, hurt received and hurt returned never balance out. The lust for vengeance only mires one more deeply in the painful unjust past. "An eye for an eye," eventually blinds us all!

Anger requires appropriate expression. It can be a positive force to generate energy to make necessary changes. It can fuel the courage it takes to make the impossible possible and the inequitable no longer acceptable. Anger is a signal that alerts the desire or the need for change. It is the right of all creatures to express. It is an emotion we must grow through if we choose to proceed towards forgiveness.

We need to find ways to let our flames fully and safely fuel themselves, without burning ourselves or igniting those around us. We need to realize that reckoning with our anger does not require us to disavow our feelings. Emotions awaken awareness and strain for accepted expression. They signal what our boundaries are and confirm we are alive. By listening to our feelings, especially to anger and tears, we gain enlightening insights that help us color in our options.

In learning to identify what sparks our angry feelings it is wise to question:
  – What red flags trigger hurt and irritability?
  – What unspoken feelings do swallowed tears conceal?
  – What unhealed sores and open wounds fester beneath lost memories?
  – Is our fiery reaction a direct response to our present circumstances? Or, is it anger vented sideways, a reaction to what this moment merely symbolizes or rekindles?

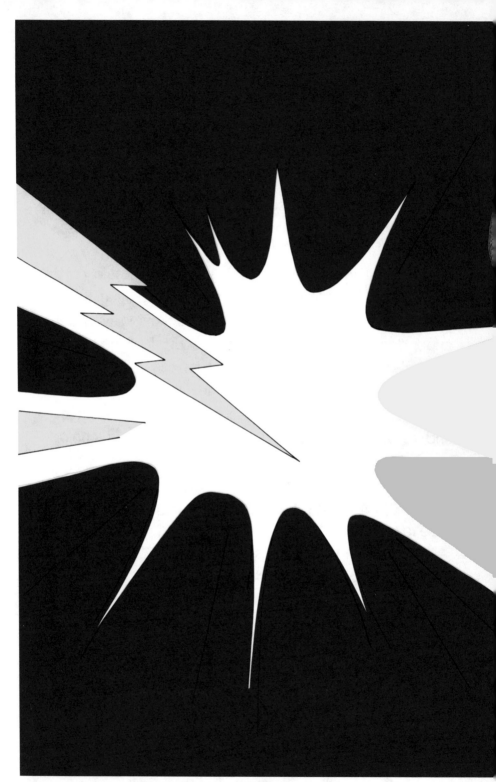

- What do the rumblings of internal thunder signal or recall?
- What imbalanced positive and negative memories do troubling nightmares reveal?
- What stormy relationships do they expose that had no rainbow endings?
- As lightning brightens the darkness, what does our anger illuminate that needs to be acknowledged or that nags to be attended?

Lightning, like anger, can be enlightening as well as frightening. We may shudder to imagine its jagged flashes slicing through our calm but thin veneer. It may seem safer to avoid acknowledging its presence or risking its expression. However, its electrical charges inevitably flash in behaviors, attitudes and moods.

My Friend, it takes more faith than most imagine not to hide when it thunders and to look honestly at uneasy truths the lightning may reveal. It takes great courage to face and move through denied and frightening feelings. There have been times in my life when I was too terrified to do that.

Following those cruel storms that lashed me, it felt safer to deny my frenzied feelings. I hoped the tears streaming down inside me would squelch the flames of grief and rage. All I could envision was a terribly changed world, a forest that held no safe place for me. My world had

betrayed me. My beliefs were all shaken. My faith was frayed and a vision of the future was fading. I had listened to the robin and tried to reroot but still I felt trapped in my feelings, like a captured mink, struggling to simply survive.

I was at the mercy of an overload of emotions I could not clearly define or control. At times I churned like a rumbling volcano about to erupt with rage. I was afraid I could no longer contain the mounting violations life had imposed. In the next second I felt like a fly wrapped in a web of restraining realities from which there seemed no escape. One moment later I felt like a defeathered bird with broken wings and no song to sing. Life had plucked every ounce of my strength. I could barely remember to breathe.

Endless, sleepless nights I lay awake, wondering if I would ever welcome the sun with energy . . . and without tears. I doubted I would ever again sing with laughter, jump with joy or outlive my fear of the wind. I could not imagine living on in the face of the unfairness I endured or ever finding ways to douse the coals of my angry sorrow. There was no justice and I could see nothing that would prompt me to ever risk loving again. I strained to listen but I could not hear the voice of Mother Earth through the ringing silence. I could not feel Her touch or sense Her presence. Sadly I feared . . . that She had moved away.

Then one otherwise uneventful day, I noticed a sweet scent in the breeze. It came from wildflowers I never noticed before that mysterious moment. It would not be until the following Winter that I would know the source of their healing fragrance. That same scent prompted an image of the owl and I awakened to a surprising realization. The storms that broke me, were now proving to be a breakthrough. Having nearly yanked all my roots raw, those awe-full storms were forcing me to see . . . I HAD TO CHANGE!!!

New awarenesses began to surface. The stream HAD been faithful. Indeed, there WERE Believers in Life who safely could be trusted. NEW sources of strength were revealing themselves to me, inviting me to respond to their presence. Some I could easily see and touch like the robin. Others were illusive, like that scent in the breeze that sought me. I began to see that if I chose to release from the angry grip of sorrow and move toward freedom, the wounded mink in the trap had to broaden its awareness and COMMIT TO CHANGE!

First, the mink had to recognize the trap that held it captive. Secondly, it had to call for others to help release its gripping stronghold. To reach for freedom, the wounded mink in the trap no longer had to struggle all alone. Enlightened with these insights, new choices became clear. With assistance, I could find freedom from my fear, my past and my pain that had trapped me in isolation.

It was an unsettling and gradual process. The vice of mixed and unnamed emotions squeezed me so tightly, my breast ached with every breath. Nonetheless, I was still breathing and dawn kept beckoning. Words of the robin echoed in my mind, "Though you cannot leave your past, you can reframe and outlive the pain it left behind. Though your sorrow once consumed you, you can learn to embrace your angry, fearful sadness and discover strength through your weakness. The day WILL COME when your pain will subside but you will still be here . . . wiser, more aware and rich with compassion."

At first it was terrifying to look at my feelings and reveal them openly to others. Surprisingly, I did not disappear when I disclosed what I was feeling, nor did those I entrusted with my pain. Relieved I discovered that courage is not being unafraid. Rather, courage is admitting we are terrified and still choosing to go on . . . not necessarily all alone. Cautiously I risked to face my brokenness and to feel my emotions . . . one . . . by . . . one. I discovered I even had the "right" to be angry!

The robin further helped me to understand my anger toward the deer. It had broken its promise of faithful friendship and left me in the middle of my misfortune. The "hurt" I felt was the only word I could find for the angry injustice I was feeling. It wasn't fair for the deer to have left

me! I trusted the deer and it chose to disappear. The robin helped me to see that "hurt" is one of many words used for the angry injustice we feel. Feelings have many names.

The wound of perceived abandonment oozed with sadness and ached for reconciliation. How could the deer run away following those cruel storms! I tried to explain how frightened and alone the storms had left me but the deer would not or could not hear me. I tried to clarify that I did not want the deer to carry my sadness. I only wanted it to faithfully stand still with me. I hoped it would allow me to lean on gentle shoulders and offer me a sense of support. However, the storms had struck me, not the deer and sadly it went away.

A band of blue jays flew to what I thought was my comfort. They had known the scent of my oldest branch and I thought that I could trust them. Their brash and raucous manner temporarily bolstered my spirits. However, my faith in them was shaken when I found they chose to break the trust I risked to place in them.

Their betrayal was revealed by the robin. Unlike the blue jays, the robin had taken "to heart" the gentler nature of the branch The Wind Shear struck. This more graceful branch had faithfully held the robin's nest secure in stormy seasons. The robin remembered her words and insight and passed them along to me:

"If one entrusts you with their confidence, receive it as a gift and as a test of your fidelity. To betray another's trust is to break the strength and the value, the spine of your word. The surest, shortest way to live with honor is to be in reality what you say and appear to be. Be care-full of the words you whisper, speak or write. Once given, they can never be retracted or erased. Therefore, speak kindly and uncritically as well as in truth. For neither endless excuses or empty apologies can recapture words once given. Hurt-full words are carried on the breeze and cut into hearts that may long to forgive . . . but sadly may never forget."

The robin stayed close to me. Strengthened by her presence and that sweet scent on the breeze, I allowed myself to own my anger, a fair response to all I had endured. I had risked to reach out to the deer and it left me! I had risked to trust the jays and they betrayed me.

Suddenly a chilling wind sliced through me. I relapsed into believing the rules and patterns from long ago must have been right. Surely, I was wrong to have reached out, to have exposed my feelings and to have risked to ask for help. Maybe the robin could not be trusted! Maybe I should go back to what was comfortable, what I had known, what I had practiced for so long, what was predictably familiar.

The winds whisked, and swirling in their midst, the ghosts of rigid routines began to howl:

"Yes, you were WRONG to question The Way of The Oaks! Now you are being PUNISHED for having risked another way! You are a FOOL to change! Go back to what you were. You are surely a loser in this game of life!"

Yes, My Friend, it takes great courage to grow and to regroove old patterns. I wept my anger and longed for the deer's return. It did not come back to me. It ran away to the evergreens to nibble on their tender, new, green shoots of growth. Was this a "punishment" I "deserved?" The blue jays banded together and eventually flew away. Was I a "fool" for having been so needy and for trusting them?

The ghosts of rigid routine were joined by the ghosts of narrow vision, old excuses and of fear. Together in a chorus they rejoiced. In that moment they held my power but in the next I took it back and I declared that THEY WERE WRONG! My anger WAS appropriate! My spirit was still INTACT! I would NOT be trapped in bitterness or believe in this kind of "justice!" I WOULD GROW IN SPITE OF ALL THE LOSS AND CONTINUE TO RISK AND TO CHANGE! Perhaps I could not totally rid myself of their intimidation but the ghosts were no longer welcome in the new life I chose to commit to create!

My Friend, we never finish with our feelings. The robin helped me accept that I could not erase the past. However, I could work towards healing the hurt that the past had left behind and draw new conclusions regarding the lessons that I learned. My challenge was to unshackle myself from recycling patterns and perceptions that burned me again and again. Life and relationships had been unfair. Paradoxically, working through my feelings and learning to forgive was the only way to fairly live with me!

This was a new kind of "justice" that surpassed the law of fairness. It was the only answer to avoid the endless reruns of recycling old hurts in my mind. Besides, if I chose not to forgive, I would skewer my own soul with the piercing desire for revenge. Gently the robin reminded me, "Mother Earth will surely guide you, reach for you and comfort you when you falter. Forgiving will NOT require a betrayal of your feelings or forgetting the pain of the past!"

At last one Spring I did not watch for the deer or the blue jays and I wished them no misfortune. Then I knew I had truly begun to forgive, to let go and to move forward. The sweet scent from the forest's new flowers wrapped around me. At long last I was free of the weight of my anger. For more than a season it had bound me to unfairnesses remembered. Released from its grasp, renewed energy emerged and fresh insights blossomed.

I realized we no longer shared a familiar forest similarly perceived or spoke the same language. Some good memories remained. However, the deer was gone as was my hope for its return. I had tried to reconnect and clarify my perceptions but still it could or would not hear me. It had been a comfort for a little while but sadly our time had passed. Occasionally the blue jays called to me from neighboring nests they built in the absence of my departed branches. I voiced my feelings with each of them and we chose to disagree respectfully. Eventually the sting of their betrayal was balanced by good times I recalled and I no longer wrestled with their presence . . . or their absence.

My Friend, sometimes friends are with us for only short seasons and sometimes friends must part. Significant relationships are not only characterized by lengthy stays, but also by lessons learned and growth nourished. Even brief encounters can mark monumental impressions. The more deeply we invest, the more difficult and often the more delayed the departure. Endings are seldom without cost, often leaving wounds that need tending and mending. A heart hungry for healing is nourished by anger and sorrow appropriately expressed and by a network of caring connections.

The robin further helped me to see that the deer's departure illuminated feelings from previous, painful farewells

and disproportioned investments. Remember, My Friend, "Every Autumn is accumulatively marked on the calendar of the soul." Perhaps I saw pieces of my lost branches in the presence of the deer and in the blue jays.

The robin continued to explain, "Those with whom we choose to connect typically are not totally unknown. It is no coincidence with whom you bond. Often we seek what is familiar, not always what is best. Sometimes we make connections to relive or to redo relationships that failed in the past. However, you are now rerooting and must be very selective. You must learn to make different connections if you want to avoid repeating cycles of heartbreak. Also, look at the patterns of behavior in those with whom you connect. More than likely, they will repeat their old routines in their new friendship with you.

The robin continued, "The blue jays are gone as is the deer and your two beloved branches. However, not to risk is to choose never to love. Not to love is to choose only to exist. Not to be angry is to live with no boundaries. Not to forgive is to commit yourself to a lifetime of fighting to even the score in what some sadly call, the game of life."

The Robin raised her breast and sternly stated, "LIFE IS NOT A GAME! If it were a game, then only one could be a winner and the rest would all be losers. There would be

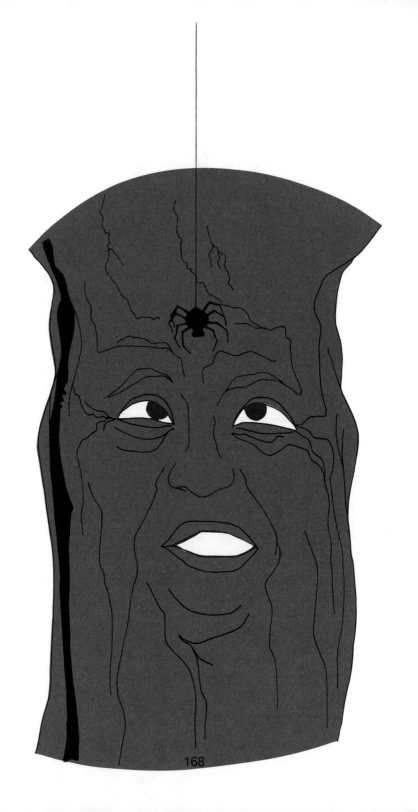

no room for friendship or for harmony. Hope would only be for the demise of one another. LIFE IS A SACRED MYSTERY MEANT TO BE SHARED. Embrace your pain and cry your tears. You have not lost YOU in any of these unchosen departures. Remember, there may be hidden gifts even in sad endings. Acorns far outlive fallen oaks. Focus on what you have gained and question:

– What changes in me do I need to make so I GROW in response to my loss, pain and sorrow?
– What have I GAINED through what I have lost?
– Now, where do I GROW from here?

"Be patient with yourself and others. Recall the wisdom the spider shared with you many seasons past. He taught you that every creature, like you, is trying to find their way in the forest that you share. However, you each perceive things uniquely. What is right for you is reversed for another. Every experience, every relationship, offers a chance to learn and to grow. Identify stale, outlived illusions, false perceptions, and reversed expectations. Remember, you cannot change another. YOU only can change YOU!

"Now is the time to release any leftover anger you may be harboring. It is an essential step in working toward forgiveness that will free you to move forward. If you do not choose to do so, you may keep pieces of your anger

wrapped and unfairly offer them as undeserved "gifts" to an unsuspecting, innocent, new friend."

At last I understood and accepted that I had lost temporary, yet still significant friends, who could not or who did not wish to share all seasons. Also, I could see that the storms from my earlier years and those of that awful Winter and Summer could become "times of my making" not only "times of demise." Then I cried a final tear for the deer and I sadly withdrew from the blue jays.

Wiser now and with altered expectations I say, "I will remember the good times we all shared. Farewell, deer friend. The miracle of your presence is now more clear to me. I thank you for the comfort that you offered. I still miss you too, you blue jays. Be kind to yourselves and to one another. I wish you all new Springtimes. As for me, I will risk to trust the stream again and watch for the sandpipers to share with me . . . joy!"

My Friend, storms are not always negative and neither are feelings we fear. At times anger is necessary and renewing. Lightning can ignite fires that clear out old brush and fallen, broken branches. Left unattended such rubble clutters the forest and inhibits new growth. Left unacknowledged, old hurts, broken boundaries and rigid patterns can litter our lives and cripple new life. Anger, like

lightning, can either fuel our growth or leave us in ashes. The choice is ours.

Remember, relationships that do not end peacefully do not truly end . . . unless . . . we finally learn to let go and hopefully . . . we learn to forgive. Choosing not to work toward this end fosters an unforgiving spirit that exhausts us with endless reruns of old rendezvous with pain.

New growth begins in the forest only after the fire is fully squelched and forgiveness reseeds the soil. We all need occasional fires and burnouts. We also need forgiveness. This includes forgiving ourselves for our poor choices and unwise investments. Within each is the seed of insight.

My Friend, releasing feelings in productive ways is like weeding a garden and plowing the soil for the planting of fresh new seeds. When we learn to appropriately express them, those feelings that most frighten us can become resourceful tools for building safe boundaries, solid con- nections and hope for Springtimes to come.

We all need occasional rain showers as well. Allowed to safely release themselves, cloud bursts, like tears, can wash away illusions and soften parched and hardened soil. Wild violets blossom and little forest critters are cleansed in the rain. Sometimes there is even a rainbow, a reminder that our faith-full Mother Earth . . . has not moved away.

SECTION IV

GIFTS RECEIVED
THROUGH LOSS

The peak of Autumn is long past. The wind has turned sharp. It orchestrates the trees in scratchy tones as barren, brown, brittle leaves crack and scrape each other. My stiffened joints creak in resistance to the blasting cold. The stream is no longer a colorful collage of floating foliage. Her icy water reflects a disrobing forest, poignantly preparing for Winter. How quickly Summer slipped away and Autumn disappeared.

I feel the nakedness of my barren branches. I shiver at the thought of bitter winds approaching. How thankful I am for your celebrated return, My Friend, and for the colorful images we tucked away of a rich Autumn shared. Recalling them will brighten the bleakness of the season ahead.

A sense of pride swells within me as I remember past seasons I feared I would not survive. Yet, here I am still standing, a worn and wiser oak. I hear the waves of birds lapping southward and am no longer washed with sadness. I trust that the same Inner Voice that maps their way to warmer days will bring them back to me next Spring. I watch tireless raccoons stuff themselves, storing fat for their long sleep through frozen days. I know inevitably that Winter is coming but I no longer resent and resist its arrival. This seasonal guest is at long last accepted.

At last I am learning to listen to what life has been trying to teach me. I am more accepting of what I cannot change and more open to receive life's uninvited guests, like Winter, who may "bare" hidden gifts. I am finally learning to focus my energies on discovering ways to grow through adversity, rather than remain angered at its arrival. No, life has not gotten easier for me, My Friend. However, I have gotten better at living.

In younger years I questioned, "When I am gone, will it have mattered that I lived?" Now I live more fully in the present and am concerned mostly if it matters that I am. At last I can say that on most days, I believe that it does. Yes, I am! And yes, my life does matter! Instead of brooding over "nothing lasts," I accept that fact as one of life's truths. Now I strive to find meaning and purpose in the transitory, in the fleeting joys that so quickly pass and in the little miracles that truly matter.

Storms have sharpened my senses and softened my humbled awareness of the sinews that connect me to the center of all life. Everything has changed. Viewing life is now like gazing through a kaleidoscope. Those shattered pieces of me are finally falling into place, revealing radiating relationships and illuminating insights. Experience has altered my beliefs and expanded my vision. Looking through this new lens has transformed everything.

I see the evergreens very differently. Viewed only through my pain, I saw them as forever free of misfortune. I was resentfully jealous of them. It seemed that I was repeatedly ravaged by ill winds and they were safely protected. I am not proud to acknowledge that I sometimes wished them less than the best.

Looking through this new lens, I no longer feel that fiery sense of injustice rage through me, clouding my view of the evergreens and of me. Having grown through grief, I see that tears and laughter are not opposites. Nor does the presence of one assure the absence of the other. With the passing of many seasons, my sobs have subsided and I hear more clearly the murmurs of others. In quiet humility I recognize and I admit my own myopic vision.

Yes, the evergreens were free of misfortune for longer than I, but in time we all are challenged. Life has now changed for them too. The hum of the bees has been silenced by the buzz of the chain saws scalping the land. Jagged teeth rip through their trunks, spewing bits of life as sawdust. Thundering echoes fill the forest as giant matriarchs and patriarchs are feverishly felled to the ground.

Their fall is softened only slightly by a thick cushion of brittle, brown needles that blanket the otherwise barren forest floor. Could these be layers of tears from the trees I

thought never cried? Yes, the evergreens must have known loss and sadness in ways I never noticed. They must have wept under the cover of darkness as the forest lay sound sleep. I wonder if they called to me for comfort but my cries drowned out their voices. I see now that we all hurt in hidden ways that others seldom see or hear.

The howling whine of chain saws rivet terror in the hearts of those who nest in the forest. There are gaping holes on the hillsides where proud pines once stood. The tall timbers that were safe homes for many, including the owl, now lay severed, stacked or destroyed. In the absence of the evergreens, the wind can have its way more easily with all of us. Now I see that those I resented once shielded and protected me in ways I never noticed.

Life is an incredible web of contradicting connections! No one of us stands alone. Persistently, Mother Earth nudges us to notice we are all a part of one another. When the dignity of a few or even one is denied, the safety of all is threatened. Hopefully, as we journey through shared seasons, we discover who our Real Family is and who we are called to become. Having known the pain of injustice myself, I am now called to raise my voice on behalf of my siblings. I must act in defense of the evergreens.

My vision of the deer too has changed. Quietly I watch it savor the scent of the cedars, still spared the pursuit of plaid jackets. I see it affectionately rub its back against the straight trunk of the spruce. Although a twinge of discomfort still churns, looking through this new lens, feelings of angry abandonment no longer surface. The deer was a great comfort to me for a little while. It was a source of temporary but very real support. Perhaps I had asked for more than the deer had to offer in friendship.

In the future maybe the deer and the blue jays will choose to reconnect with me. Then again, maybe they will not. Whatever their decisions, I have chosen to look elsewhere for friendship. Foolish are those who dip from wells that have no water. Frustrated are those who pound on doors that have no hinges. One cannot give what he does not have. Refusing to accept what will not likely occur, digs our rut more deeply and elevates frustrating disappointment.

Perhaps success is getting what one wants and happiness is accepting and making the most of what one has. Surely, seeing is not believing. BELIEVING IS SEEING. My world and my life are happier now, viewed through this transforming lens. My beliefs have broadened. My vision has expanded. I have grown through sad endings, empty wells and closed, locked unhinged doors.

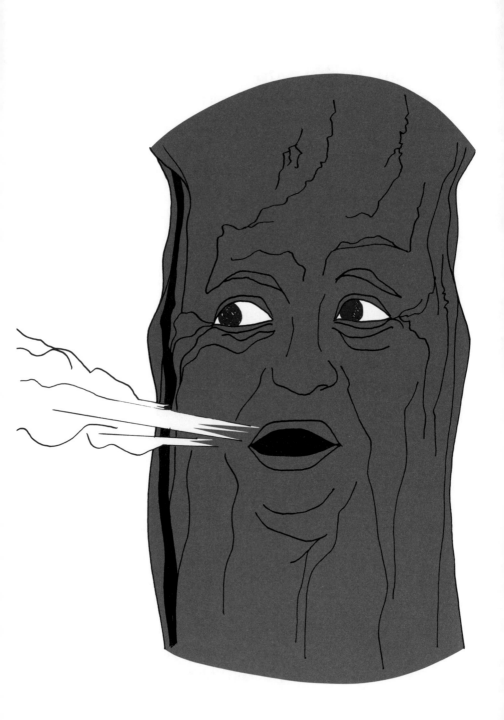

My Friend, you may have noticed that the last chapter in *Grow Deep Not Just Tall* was the shortest. It was the chapter titled, Winter, The Season of Patience and of Growth. It was the most difficult for me to write about because it was the most difficult for me to accept, much less appreciate. Patience takes so long to learn and its gifts are so well hidden. Yet, Winter, like learning, must not be rushed. In the seasons of waiting, the seeds of humility and wisdom are sown.

My Friend, I had to live more of Winter to understand its meaning. I had to face the cold squarely, stop running and listen. I had to stand still for what seemed an eternal Winter. In silence, I had to confront those shadows in the snow. Waiting quietly, I finally experienced that healing and growth do come . . . but only in their due time.

Standing still in the shimmering moonlight, I focused on the glistening filigrees of frost that sparkled like dia-monds on my regal snow gown. Opening my senses fully to the present, I released thoughts of yesterday and concerns for tomorrow. Patiently, Mother Earth waited with me until I realized it was HER breath breathing through me as it does through all of life. Only in Winter could I have seen what I saw in that moment. Only icy breezes could reveal Her visible breath. We miss so much when we fail to wait!

Look, My Friend, the nights are stretching farther into the mornings these days. Temperatures have plunged and so has my willingness to stay separated and alone, obsessing on what is beyond my influence or control. Mother Earth has taught me to act more responsibly and to take better care of myself, especially in the Winter. Her fidelity has proven itself unconditional, a source of strength and of joy as well. Continually, She prompts me to reach beyond what I know and discover life anew all around me. Like a Wise Woman in the center of my soul, I sense Her spiritedness within me. I can feel Her tickling humor, lifting me above serious, heavy contemplation, and prompting me to celebrate each moment.

I call for my friends, the squirrels, to come play with me. I no longer passively wait for them to sense my loneliness. I do more than coyly hint my needs. Winter has taught me it is better to risk expressing my desires, than choose to stay alone pouting, angered because others have not guessed what I want or need. Patiently, I wait and hope the squirrels will respond. True invitations are never demands.

They come, announcing their arrival with flickering tails and typical boundless energy. Twitching their whiskers, they sit back on their haunches and playfully clown for attention. Their laughter is contagious. Their spirits are uplifting. How shallow life would be without a few

190

squirrely friends who joyfully, freely love life! Zigzagging along my stiffening limbs, they dodge one another's attempted tags and the first fluffy snowflakes that try to nestle in their fur. Yes, Winter is here again.

Soon I will relive another season riddled with indelibly difficult dates. No doubt, some memories will surface of those bitter Night Winds of Winter long past. They never fail to unveil vulnerability. However, I move through them more gracefully than I did in years past. I accept they will recycle, year after year. I no longer fear or avoid them. I have learned to move forward with them and to reclaim the power they once wielded over me.

As more seasons have slipped between those pain-filled first anniversaries and today, the sadness has softened and happier memories have surfaced. Of course, they are still poignant, but over time those threads of heart-break have been intimately woven into the tapestry of my being. I have come to accept their presence and to cherish the compassion they have added to the texture of my soul. Winter is no longer an unwelcomed guest.

These long, cold nights can be lonely. They also have become times for reflection and occasionally times of very good fortune. In the darkest nights the northern lights are most visible. They glisten like the long shining cylinders of a pipe organ in the sky. Intricate forms are silhouetted on the snow, as light filters through my branches and those of my neighbors. Our forms intermingle and patterns appear, revealing relationships we might never have noticed, had not Winter forced us to pause and reflect.

Like the breath of the buffalo on a cold December dawn, life is fleeting, ever-changing and mystically uncontainable. Now rather than respond with resistance to the inevitable cold, Winter has given me the gift of insight-full awareness and grace-full acceptance. I stand quietly, accepting Winter.

My Friend, nonresistance is not necessarily giving IN or giving UP our power. Rather, it can be choosing to trust Mother Earth and giving OVER to Her time wasted in worry and resentment. Releasing anxiety and extending my patience, I allow Her breath to warm and strengthen me. Trusting Her, I stand relaxed and grounded. Reconnected with my tap root, I can face the winds with an attitude of anchored acceptance and with faith that holds firm in an Empowering Presence.

Silhouetted shadows on the snow reveal mirrored images that tell stories, not with words but with shapes that speak eloquently of storms survived and prices paid. Wrapped in the blanketing white of Winter, we see our connections with one another and hear our hearts beating in similar rhythms. In our loneliness we are indeed all so much together. What a comforting and fortunate insight! We are not all alone in the night.

One December midnight I received a most amazing gift. I was staring at my frail reflection in the snow, wondering if my gnarled, old arms reaching heavenward would ever embrace you or another once again. I knew I had to keep extending myself and striving to become the friend I longed to find. My Friend, it was not easy, for my joints were stiff and my limbs were tired. Nonetheless, I chose to keep waiting, believing and reaching. When I least expected a change to occur, a welcomed guest arrived.

I could not see who it was but I could hear the flapping of weary wings approaching. I was startled to feel the uneven landing of a long-departed friend, the owl. His wing was nearly broken by a hunter's cruel bullet. Another deadly shot had broken the owl's heart by silencing the voice of his mate for-all-seasons. Wandering aimlessly in the darkness of despair, the owl had seen my gnarled, old branches and came to rest safely with me.

My Friend, I am sorry you never met the owl. However, the proper timing for special encounters seems to be mystically arranged. Like the seasons, they are not always of our choosing or within our control or demand. I knew the owl long before you and I discovered one another. Years had come between us but the warmth of our friendship never waned. It is true, "There is no distance or measure of time that can separate the freeing bond of love."

Frightened and alone the owl searched for the shelter of familiar, safe places. The tall evergreens that once had been "home" now lay splintered and stacked on the floor of the forest. Guided through his sadness by a faint but faithful breeze, he glided through the shadows and came to rest with me.

At first I hardly recognized him. He was so changed, so different than I remembered. In my youth he appeared regal, almost professor-like. He had always sat tall, proudly perched on my strong and eager young limbs. He looked as wise as his reputation yet sometimes austere, as if he possessed secrets selfishly shielded.

Those who knew him in years past each perceived him uniquely. The field mice trembled at the thought of his talons and saw him as a monster to be feared. The deer timidly watched him and stood frozen when their eyes

locked in silent stares. The squirrels winked back at him and playfully chattered silly names when he seriously called, "Whooo?" The evergreens bowed in his presence and were proud to be his nesting choice. I too had stood in awe of his air of elegance and marveled that the squirrels had such nerve to tease him. However, that night in the pale moonlight sat the form of a very changed owl.

He looked fragile, lonely and afraid. His shadowed, shivering form looked as tired and worn as I felt before he landed. Strange as it may sound, feeling his trembling weight resting on me, filled me with renewed strength. Of all he might have flown to in the forest that night, he sought and chose to trust me. I felt warmed inside, happy, yet humbled, thrilled that the owl had returned.

We did not speak. Clouds drifted past the moon and I slipped into thoughts of the owl I had known. His presence in my younger years had remained a lasting influence on me. In his absence I often thought of him and of his few, measured words. Always they were kind, inviting me to extend past perceived limits and to look beyond the obvious for truth.

He had modeled patience and quiet insight in the brief seasons we shared. He would swoop through silent nights with a slice of moonlight on his wings and always

200

landed precisely where he planned. Although he nested in the evergreens, I was often his chosen perch. Naively, I questioned what he saw in me, a small, unseasoned oak tree. Sometimes his presence intimidated me. At the same time I felt more secure when he was near. Winter's dawn was more believable as we awaited its arrival in shared solitude.

The owl spoke of potential he saw in the zest of my spirit and of faith that he held in my future. I felt a mixture of embarrassment and pride that one so wise would favor me. I was not as graceful as the willows or breathtaking like the pines. Unable to see what he saw in me and incapable of truly believing him, I tucked his words safe inside me, like a gift I was not worthy of receiving. Then one night he went away and with him, I thought, went the source of life's wisdom. I was wrong.

Indeed, he had much to teach me, and I grew in response to his presence. His faith in me took root and led me to believe in more than I ever imagined before his kindness touched me. However, his wisdom was his treasure that he could only share. He could not give it directly to me or to any other. His answers were his as were his insights. He could only encourage and assist me to search for and to discover my own.

My Friend, as the soul hungers for meaning and connections, it also thirsts for understanding and for truth. Wisdom is to vision as dawn is to darkness. It is brighter than the glow of black and white answers and illuminates truth beyond brittle right and wrong. Wisdom is a gift wrapped in experience. Neither measured by years or guaranteed in longevity, seasoned-wisdom is vision tempered with love. It channels through our Inner Voice that speaks in the seed of our center. It sees connections beyond reason. The light of wisdom glimmers when our soul's eye is opened and we begin to focus on and to learn "by heart" what is most important.

In the absence of the owl, his vision of me and his words loomed on, especially during dark times when I questioned my value, my strength, my roots and the meaning of "gifts of the lightning." In the darkest night of my soul, the owl spoke to me in a dream. Do you remember, My Friend, when that was? It was not long after The Wind Shear severed my cord to life and left me beyond consolation. Exhausted, I fell into a deep sleep and in that most grievous night I felt the voice of the owl resonate within me, "There is not always justice, only love."

Yes, My Friend, we are shaped by those who do and do not believe in us. We are formed by those who love and those who refuse to love us. Ultimately we are who we

choose to become in response to the voices we hear and believe.

Wise are those who listen to robins and owls, to spiders and squirrels. Through their voices and those of count-less others, we hear Mother Earth who never forces or forsakes us. In each season, through all events, and within every relationship, She calls our name and invites us to learn and to grow. With each sunset and every good-bye, She renews Her promise to hold us safely through the night, to keep us grounded in Her love. With each new day, She invites us to rediscover the depend-able dawn and the invincible sun in our soul.

The night the owl returned to me, insights were ignited that I had long awaited. For years I had wondered what seeds he saw in me. That night I could see some of their blossoms, silhouetted in our shadows on the snow. Life had changed as it inevitably does, and we each were still choosing to grow through it all. Obviously, life had taken its toll on us both, but prices must always be paid. Noth-ing comes for free, especially growth and love.

The owl fluffed his feathers to warm himself and flinched when his wounded wing moved. The agony of his grief and the anguish in his eyes echoed in my own broken heart. I could not enter into all he felt or bear the burden

of his pain. I could only offer my love, the strength of my caring and the affection of one seeking to understand the storm-swept barrenness of so great a loss. When the time was right I would whisper his words back to him, words that sustained me and carried me beyond reason, beyond bitterness . . . to hope. "THERE IS NOT ALWAYS JUSTICE . . . ONLY LOVE!"

The owl sat still in the safety of my support. Shielding my wounded friend, I began to sense deeper understandings of "Winter, The Season of Patience and of Growth." Resting together, we were warmed by each other's concern and in awe of each other's growth. In silence, I reflected on all the Winters I could recall. I began to see there are indeed limits to patience's productiveness and that there is a fine line between letting go and holding on. Patience that is seasoned is not passive. It is balanced. It requires releasing others to make and to own their own choices. Similarly, it does not demand draining anticipation that the fox will cleverly one day learn to fly. Yes, there are many pieces of Autumn's letting go in Winter's call for patience.

My Friend, it takes two hearts to thaw friendship that has frozen and experience to broaden our vision. Sadly, sometimes there is no mutual thaw or shared enlightenment. It takes time and maturity to accept that there are not always happy endings. Yet, there may be new beginnings even in

the endings we might never choose. Had I waited forever for the return of the deer, I might never have met the robin, rediscovered the owl . . . or found my own, lost little acorn.

My Friend, love releases what must go. Hope watches for green shoots to reach through frozen soil. Faith believes in the future. Sometimes friends must part so that each can hopefully grow. Then perhaps at another time, in another season or in Another Place . . . they may bid one another a mutually respect-full and welcomed, "Hello Again." That wintry midnight marked such a reunion for two changed and seasoned souls. The owl and I reconnected.

I was no longer a young sapling tentatively reaching out to life. I was weathered, worn and deeply rooted. The seeds of potential the owl saw slumbering in my young timbers had matured. Through adversity I had become the spirited oak he believed I one day would become. The owl too had changed. Like the field mice who once feared him, the owl had learned humbling vulnerability. Now his eyes locked with mine in silent stares as they once did with the deer's. In time the owl's laughter would break through his tears and the squirrels would teach him how to be play-full.

Like myself and the evergreens and so many of our sisters and brothers, the owl was struggling to find safety and new meaning in our forest forever changed. Meaning-fully

connected, we would search to find our way. Together we would continue to learn "By Heart" how to become "more" in the face of loss and still believe in the promise of Spring.

My Friend, life holds more secrets than we can uncover on our own. Mother Earth calls us to share in our journeys, to find our way HOME and discover our . . . REAL FAMILY. She reminds us that there is not enough time for any of us to unwrap all that is hidden in mystery or to see the fullness that truth would reveal. Those who love know wisely that we are connected far beyond the seen and measured horizon. So power-full is LOVE that there MUST be more than the limits of a few brief cycles of seasons for its full expression. Those who love deeply, SURELY never see or touch each other for the last and final time. Love is NEVER lost, My Friend. It is only transformed.

The owl sat stooped on my broken branch. Shrouded in silence, I glimpsed his glowing eyes, their centers as black and piercing as the private moments of despair we each had known. The golden windows to his soul slowly disappeared behind quivering lids and tears trickled undisclosed feelings. In my youth I never thought the owl would ever cry. I never imagined he would ever have need of me. Life and love are always more than we can fully fathom.

I had always dreamed that maybe one day I might be just half as knowledgeable as the owl. I thought perhaps then I might be a portion of what he hoped I would become. Perhaps if I grew straight and strong, I too might have a sense of elegance about me and resemble the owl I respected. Maybe then he would return and be proud of this oak. I was amazed to discover it was none of these that drew him home to the tree of his choice.

It was my gnarled branches that he saw as seasoned by life's inevitable storms and shaped with raw character. Though barren and broken, he saw them as yellow-ribboned invitations offering weathered acceptance. My trunk was no longer straight and it was scarred. It leaned to one side exposing some of my roots. The owl saw it as weighted with experience and firmly rooted in the solid soil of Mother Earth who birthed us both.

The long shining cylinders of the pipe organ in the sky chimed in joyful celebration of our reconnection. Harsh winds had nearly broken my spirit and my hope for love's return. Those same winds had caused me to reroot. They had served to strengthen my courage. In response to their force, I had risked to become who life challenged and called me to be. A gentler version of those same winds had buoyed the weary, broken wings of the owl. They glided him safely back to me.

214

Our reunion that night was a poignant homecoming. Sadly, I had never met the owl's mate but he had known my beloved branches torn away by the storms. At a later time he would reveal where they had gone. The owl had come to comfort as well as to be comforted. In giving a gift we also receive. In receiving a present we can also give. That frozen night in the darkness, the flame to faith was rekindled. Two gave and two received.

Snowflakes melted in the tears on his cheeks and the owl crawled into the hole in my trunk. The hollowed wounds gouged by the Night Winds of Winter and Wind Shear of Summer were now lined with tender compassion. Wounds I had angrily resented and once feared would forever be filled with only sorrow had become an inviting, safe harbor for my grieving broken friend.

The northern lights glowed softly and the snowflakes ceased. I could feel the warmth of the owl's sighs and an icy breeze carried our blended breaths in the moonlight. Leaning against one another, the owl and I received a most precious gift. It was the gift of presence, the presence of one who faith-fully waits with us for the dawn to come again . . . and hope-fully anticipates new seasons to celebrate.

216

I wonder where the white goes when Winter's snow is gone. I wonder where warm winds begin before they start to blow. I wonder why some billow, even bully, and blow in gales, while others gently, softly soothe and caress. My Friend, I wonder, can we truly separate one season from another or safely see ourselves as divided from each other? Are we not all important pieces of The Whole, each subject to the wind, all choosing how we will or will not grow? Life is such a paradox, a mystery not a game, not a problem to be solved with simple answers.

Now I see that New Beginnings indeed do Fully blossom if we Patiently learn to Let Go. Mysteries and new meanings are carried in the breath of the breeze, far exceeding the measures of mind and matter and of our perceptions of "justice." Yes, Mother Earth does keep Her promises! She nurtures Autumn's acorns into giant Summer oaks. She never allows a Winter without the hope of Spring.

My Friend, the owl and I grew deeper during that long cold wintry season. Beneath the blankets of black velvet skies and soft white snows, we slept, as did the feisty little field mice snuggled safely in their burrows. Healing and growth both take time and require segments of quiet. Rooted securely in Mother Earth and sensing our sacred tap roots, the owl and I risked to close our eyes

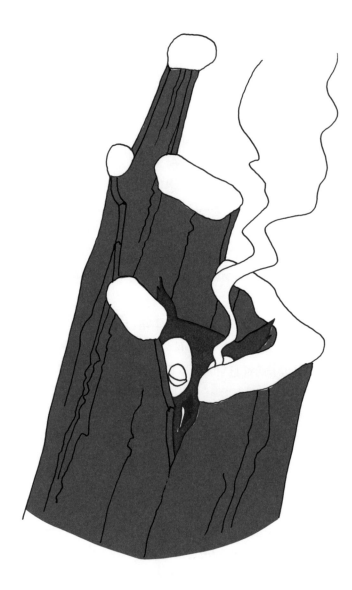

and trust the presence of each other. Cautiously, in the soft glow of crisp, white moonlight, we risked to share our stories. We exposed our hurts to one another and our gnawing questions that had no simple answers.

We discovered that our stories were similar yet unique in detail. Our questions overlapped. Neither of us held the other's answers. We found we were more alike than different from each other. Surprisingly, we discovered more of ourselves, the more we trusted and risked to reveal. Paradoxically, the more we gave, the more we received!

Soothingly, we salved our sadness in the shelter of each other's support. Neither of us could take away the void in the bottom of our broken hearts or remove the ache of loneliness. Bullets, storms and nightmares come true had carved indelible marks on the calendars of our souls. Our "accumulated Autumns" would forever be with us. Nonetheless, life was now challenging us to rebraid our frayed strands and step forward toward tomorrow.

Though we loved each other, we could not banish the threat of yet more tragedy or take away the shadow of one another's grief. Nor could we guarantee "forever" friendship in this ever changing forest. We knew all too well that one day we might not watch the sun rise, standing safely, side-by-side. In the end, the best we could do was faithfully hold each other in the luminous darkness and consistently

confirm our compassionate presence. We could choose to believe in life that surpasses reason and reach out to love again. That had to be enough, for it was the most that anyone can offer.

My Friend, risking to connect deeply in moments of naked honesty, joy or sorrow, rekindles our hunger to be rewrapped in the womb of unconditional acceptance and total knowing. However, the ultimate intimacy that our minds mystically recall from before our birth is only momentarily revisited, here in our seasoned forest. The owl and I had to gradually accept that neither of us could offer or attain unaltered security. Life and relationships constantly change, despite protests, illusions or unrelenting denials. Life and intimacy are daring adventures with few absolute assurances.

Sharing peak moments or passionate pinnacles temporarily erase estrangement. They reattach us to our centers that we lose touch with as we wander from our essence and compete with one another. Such unifying moments and climaxing connections are tucked between before and after. Relished in the NOW and savored in memory, moments of intimacy can be both wonder-full and terrifying. They may be fulfilling in the present, ultimately exhilarating. However, those same moments may also be sources of loneliness and even remorse when replayed through euphoric recall or objectivity.

When we risk to touch and to be touched, we can be changed by the contact. When these encounters are grounded with reverent respect, we may discover a sense of our sacred selves and of who we are called to be. Such home-comings are seldom solitary experiences. More typically, they are relationship reunions. The gift of genuine intimacy feeds The Spirit that hungers for connections and that strains to grow and to become MORE. If on our journeys our paths join and ultimately, empoweringly, undulate . . . that is cause. . . . . . TO CELEBRATE!

In hushed voices as Winter waned, the owl and I entrusted more and more of our sacred stories. Neither of us believed The Cycler of Seasons had destined the pain we had come to know. However, we wondered if perhaps in freeing us to choose our own paths, Mother Earth was wisely inviting us to feel our loneliness and hopefully to discover our longing and our need for one another.

In the chill of an early wintry morning a single blackbird took flight and announced the dawn. Morning had broken the darkness of night. In the very same moment, our souls' eye was opened and the owl and I could see ourselves in each other's image. Mystically a voice spoke through our hearts and in our hesitant glances that shyly sought connection. A sense of the sacred was mirrored through one another and our hearts could hear what the voice was saying.

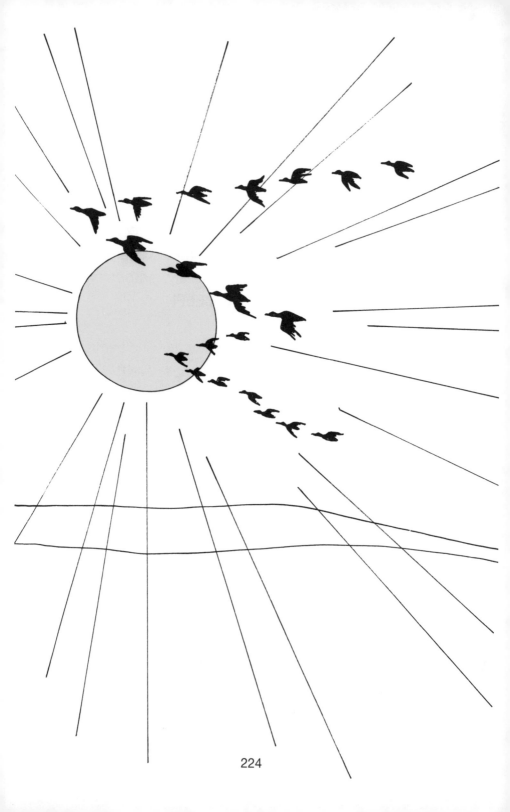

224

The voice called to each of us through one another . . . but without words. It was Real yet uncontainable, like the single breath we saw floating between us. In the language of the soul the voice spoke:

"I am hungry for understanding . . .
   Lavish me with acceptance.
   Nourish me with kindness.
   Teach me how to till, to sow, to harvest.
I am naked of dignity . . .
   Clothe me with respect.
   Speak out on my behalf.
   Help me, require me to own responsibility.
I am homeless, orphaned and abandoned . . .
   Do not betray me.
   Warm me in the comfort of your compassion.
   Buoy me on the breath of your belief in me."

We stood still in the presence of such a mystery. A quiet, transforming awareness filled us with a sense of reverence for all of life and for one another. Beyond our capacities to reason or to explain we KNEW more than we had ever known and it changed the lens we looked through.

Gradually the sun rose higher on the horizon and embranced us with warm healing rays. Winged waves of southern travelers lapped their way home . . . and so did the owl and I, in the harbor of our friendship. The moon grew larger and

nights drew shorter. On that first bright morning of Spring, two All-Seasons-Friends found TRUE FAMILY.

The comfort I initially offered my wounded friend in the beginning of that Winter was gifted back to me again and again as the owl shared more of himself with me. Although he was not with me when The Night Winds tore my oldest branch, amazingly he had seen where it had gone. Nested high in the evergreens, shielded from the storm, the owl saw the old branch pass beneath him. Bitter gusts had sent it skidding along the frozen stream. Trapped in a bend, it was freed only when Winter finally faded away.

The solid sheets of ice that had locked her banks began to thaw, and the owl saw the stream begin to ripple. Gently she embraced the old branch in the safe caress of her current and carried it along with soothing rhythms. She reshaped and transformed all its rough and rigid edges. Finally the old branch washed ashore. Playful, prancing sandpipers hopped along its grace-full spine. The old branch had become a lovely piece of driftwood adorning the rippling shore.

The owl also knew what had become of my most beloved branch, the one The Wind Shear shattered. Its many indistinguishable pieces had showered down from the heavens. Transformed, they were now the fragrant centers of budding wildflowers that danced in the soft

Spring breeze. The essence of my beloved branch had NOT been destroyed. Like the old branch the Night Winds had taken, and like all of life, it had NOT been lost . . . only changed! The love that was our TRUE CONNECTION lived on, revealed in new forms.

How grateful I was that the storms that struck me had spared the evergreens. Perhaps the owl would not have seen my beloved branches had the evergreens been beaten as was I. Then, embarrassingly, I recalled my anger and my jealousy toward my sturdy, spared, green siblings. In earlier seasons their safety from the bitter winds had ignited my ire over unreasoned injustice. Then a voice inside me whispered, "Learn from the past and forgive yourself. Now speak on behalf of your siblings. Soon the buzz of the chain saws will scream in the forest and silence the hum of the bees."

The nights became shorter and the days longer. The field mice crept cautiously from their burrows. They yawned and stretched in the sunny rays as did the lean raccoons rolling out of their dens. Tillers of the soil recycled the warming earth. Long, slender, green grasses gracefully swayed in the breeze. A fawn struggled to stand. The robin winked at the blue jays. Spirited squirrels leaped joy-fully from one budding branch to another, each laden with clusters of new acorns. Crickets fiddled a concert and the forest sang in celebration of new beginnings of growth. The scent of Spring flowers was everywhere!

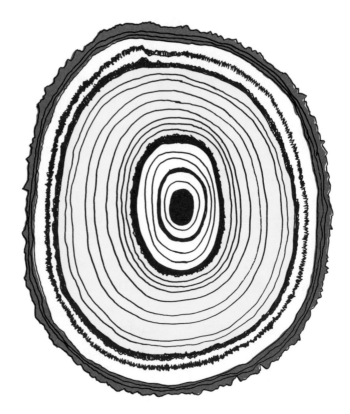

My Friend, we have grown through many seasons. One blends into the other like the strands of a braid. It is not possible to separate them without spoiling how beautifully they flow together. We too are a blend of so many pieces. Some of our needs are still out of season. Some of our wounds still ache to be healed. So many buds still await to be blossomed.

We are all weavers. Our lives are the looms, revealing the creation of our choices. Changes have caused us to reach for new threads. New patterns appear woven by the choices we have made. Contrasting colors retain their uniqueness yet blend in respect-full harmony. Each is a sacred part of the Weaver of All Seasons and a piece of each other's tapestry.

My Friend, the rings within my core, like the lines that grace your face, chart the seasons we have grown through and the patterns we have grooved. Each is filled with memories that tell segments of our stories. Together we have worked to heal the hurts the past left behind and to learn from the lessons change has taught us. We have discovered, as surely as Spring follows Winter, we too can bring life out of bleak, barren seasons . . . of sorrow, loss, and pain. Now we must continue to plant the seeds of new life and to care for this forest that we share.

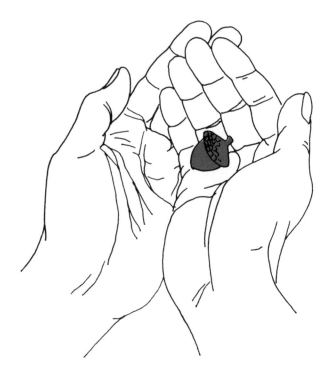

Life is far beyond measure or our imaginations. Count-less forests are hidden within a single tiny acorn. Who could fathom the beauty concealed in the dull, brown chrysalis? Who would have ever guessed that the wounds of nightmares come true could become safe harbors of compassion for the owl and open invitations for more home-comings!

My Friend, the eyes cannot see the whole of who we are. All the raw materials for true greatness are present within us, just as we are, right now in this moment. All the mystery of our Forever Child lives on deep inside us. It yearns to be tended and mended. That natural, creative, childlike spirit must be nurtured by who we are today, for it connects us to the seed in our sacred center and to The Source of our tap root. It is our Forever Child who joins us to The Great Spirit whose breath we feel in the breeze, whose scent we smell in the wildflowers, whose voice we hear in the thun-der, whose reflection we see in the stream.

Before it learned fear, our Forever Child openly embraced life. Before it learned competition, our Forever Child believed in its preciousness and felt no shame in longing for connec-tions. It made no apology for tears and reached for others' hands to hold. With respect-full curiosity it admired the uniqueness of others and valued the gifts each had to offer. It marveled at the mystery sown by the tillers of the soil.

My Friend, none of us was treated as fairly or loved nearly as fully as we longed to be treated and treasured. Too few of us choose to make peace with our past and to let go of what hinders our happiness. Allowing ourselves to face our truths, to feel our pain and to reach for new threads are the first steps in reweaving snarled strands in our looms. As surely as Autumn precedes Winter, we must learn to let go of what fragments our call to Wholeness.

I am continuing to learn how to do that. How grateful I am for the robin's guidance in rediscovering my lost little acorn, my own Forever Child. The robin taught me to cherish that child of yesterday that still lives within me today. Increasingly, I am learning to listen to that sense of The Sacred within me that never ever dies. I am learning to tend to my brokenness, to reconcile with self, to thank-fully celebrate the magic of each season.

More responsibly and care-fully, I chide myself when poor choices are made, as opposed to imposing shame. I have discovered there is much more freedom when safe boundaries are clearly, consistently defined. I embrace my fears more tenderly as opposed to denying or ignoring their presence. I laugh more openly and readily at my mistakes. In response to the squirrels' advice, I take myself less seriously. The Child within us is more safely at "home" when we lovingly learn . . . to parent . . . ourselves.

The red-breasted harbinger of Spring was one of many who helped me birth new beginnings. The spider, the squirrels, the stream, and the owl each taught me something new about life, about themselves, about me. I also grew through my connections with the winds, the blue jays, the sandpiper and the deer. Remember, what we learn largely depends on what we look for and what we choose to believe and to embrace.

I vividly recall those days I could not believe my branches would ever again bear acorns or that you would ever return. I was angry that there were no answers for my questions and I wondered what meanings might ever come through injustices gouged in sad memories. Yet, the dawn dependably arrived and hope was rebirthed every morning. Now, amazingly we are together, celebrating fresh new beginnings.

Cocoons are bursting with transforming symbols that flutter like rainbows aloft on the breeze. Their presence recalls a gift I received from the caterpillar. She was inching her path along on my limb on her way towards our shared destiny. Short and plump, shy and kind, I saw her as beauty-full. Her spirit was childlike. Her friendship I cherished. I sensed hidden treasures in her, like those the owl once saw in me. She could not believe what I honestly saw but tucked my perceptions safe inside her. The day we parted she gave to me this gift of her poem in thanks for the friendship we shared. It touched me deeply and it moved me to tears.

Her words challenged me to never underestimate the power of even a brief encounter. I had not realized how important my friendship was to this gentle, shy creature. Her poem also humbled me for it prompted me to realize I had sensed only a small portion of the immeasurable treasures The Great Spirit had tucked inside the caterpillar. Now I offer her poem to you, My Friend, for gifts are meant to be shared.

As we renew our friendship, the words of the caterpillar invite us to identify what we offer one another, what we look for in each other and what we hope will be discovered in ourselves.

The Gift

I can give you things to use and toss away,
   objects of finished beauty to touch,
   see, admire, to dust.
I can send you exotic flowers and fruits out
   of season, that die as they arrive.
   I can fashion for you responses to the wonders
   of hand and mind, art, music, clay or paint,
   or . . .
I can give you THE GIFT OF MYSELF, crudely formed,
   never finished, with needs out of season,
   ever fumbling, searching, as though Someone
   learning, practiced on me while planning
   the universe, then sidetracked, leaving
   the discovery of me . . . up to you.

My Friend, within every relationship, in every experience, there are lessons to be learned, gifts that are given
and seeds that are sown as results of our choices. Eventually stormy seasons challenge all of us and in time life
asks each of us this question:

WHAT DO YOU CHOOSE TO LEARN AND BELIEVE
ESPECIALLY WHEN SEASONS ARE NOT OF YOUR CHOOSING?
THERE IS NOT ALWAYS JUSTICE – ONLY LOVE.
LIFE IS CHANGE – GROWTH IS OPTIONAL
WILL YOU CHOOSE TO GROW?

My Friend, our forest is threatened by more than the chain
saws and not only the evergreens are endangered. Our
whole forest family is at risk if we fail to act on behalf of our
siblings. Stars struggle to shine in the heavens. Too often
they are clouded by doubt and despair. Perhaps those
stars are the souls of those who have gone before us,
those who call us to choose to change, to reunite with
what brings hope and healing . . . and life . . . to each of us!

Future seasons depend on our decisions made today.
Spring, this season of new beginnings, challenges us to
reinvest in our forest, to make a healing difference in our
lonely, wounded world. Mother Earth is nudging Her
children to once again learn to celebrate the healing
powers of laughter, love and compassion.

My Friend, is not time, even as love is, . . . beyond division and interconnecting? Yet, in our thoughts if we must measure time into segments, let each season encircle all the other seasons. May today embrace the past with memories that lead to growth. Let us live this moment so it nurtures a faith in the future and a longing for shared new beginnings.

As we rekindle our friendship this Spring, let us continue to keep the promises we made in our renewed contract of friendship. May we strive to discover the gifts of each season, of ourselves and of one another. Let us seek the wisdom of our elders, the spirit of our Forever Child and The Voice that calls our names.

My Friend, rerooted in the solid soil of Mother Earth's universal truths, may we willingly reach out to embrace the whole of life, knowing full well that not only branches but hearts will surely be broken as we risk to love again. May we help each other dare to become all we can be to make a healing difference in the forest that we share. Life is a journey through all of the seasons, a journey meant to be shared. It is all the more meaning-full when we cycle through each season hand-in-hand, committed to Grow Deep Not Just Tall. Welcome Home, My Cherished Friend. Oh, how I have missed you!

... not the end . . . to be continued ...

CEP PUBLICATIONS
BOOKS

A Trilogy of Growth

Written by Karen Kaiser Clark, these three books are inter-twined. From differing perspectives and in a natural progression, each book invites the reader to discover how growth can flourish if one chooses to change.

Where Have All The Children Gone?
Gone to Grown-Ups, Everyone!

Delightfully illustrated and appealing to all ages, this book looks at the adult world through the eyes of a child. It challenges us to see maturity not as a goal to be achieved but as a continuous process of growth to be experienced. It invites the reader to rediscover the child within.

Grow Deep, Not Just Tall

A wise and weathered oak tree teaches us how to grow through each of the seasons of our lives. It challenges us to change and grow.

Life is Change — Growth is Optional

Having survived cruel storms that threatened to destroy her, the oak tree "grows deeper" in the face of misfortune. She learns how to ask for help, to reroot, to reach out and to risk to embrace life once again. Powerfully illustrated, this book is a source of hope and comfort for those striving to grow through the unfair seasons of their lives.

TAPES
Audio Cassette Tapes
Featuring Karen Kaiser Clark

Where Have All The Children Gone?
A reading of the book and a 60 minute development of the characteristics of ever-increasing maturity.

Grow Deep, Not Just Tall
A 90 minute reading of the book accompanied with music.

Life is Change — Growth is Optional
A 60 minute presentation on the symbolic meanings of the seasons of our lives.

For information on Karen Kaiser Clark as a keynote speaker or consultant for your organization or convention, contact CEP, 13119 Heritage Way, St. Paul, Minnesota 55124. Telephone: 612/454-1163.

This is the third book in The Trilogy of Growth by author, Karen Kaiser Clark. Once again she has found the words to magically create another source of hope, humor, healing and comfort for readers of all ages. Complimented with the delightful illustrations by Larry Anderson, words, colors, symbols and textured expressions are sensitively woven into a masterful manuscript.

Karen Kaiser Clark is as warm and approachable as she appears. A former teacher, Karen now lectures and conducts seminars internationally. A popular keynote speaker addressing the broad area of human relations, Karen has earned her reputation as a real professional who shares who she is as well as what she has learned. Karen graduated with honors from Western Michigan University and went on to do graduate work in psychology at the Universities of Michigan and Minnesota. She served as a consultant for the Minnesota Department of Education and has conducted workshops in as far away places as The Philippine Islands and Okinawa. Karen is president of The Center of Executive Planning. Having grown through personal tragedies herself, Karen is often called upon by staffs and organizations facing painful realities. Describing herself as no expert but rather as "one woman with ideas to share," she challenges her audiences to nurture their sense of humor and creatively find ways to make the very most of the fragile gift of life, themselves and one another. Karen resides in Minnesota with her husband, Lou, and their two children Kelli and Kevin.

Larry W. Anderson is a sculptor and painter living in Bonney Lake, Washington, with his wife, Sharilyn, and their third child Caplan. A graduate of Central Washington State University, Larry received his Master of Fine Arts from Cranbrook Art Academy in Bloomfield Hills, Michigan. He has studied at the Academy of Fine Art in Vienna. Widely acclaimed for his life-sized bronze sculptures depicting themes of relationship, Larry is a long time, personal friend of the author. The quote inscribed in Larry's portfolio well describes this gentle man, "We do what we can. We give what we have."